# CONTENTS

Gu Hua

# A Small Town Called Hibiscus

Translated by Gladys Yang

Panda Books

Panda Books
First Edition 1983
Reprinted 1987, 1990
Copyright 1983 by CHINESE LITERATURE PRESS
ISBN 0-8351-1074-5
ISBN 7-5071-0021-9/I.22

Published by CHINESE LITERATURE PRESS, Beijing (37), China
Distributed by China International Book Trading Corporation
21 Chegongzhuang Xilu, Beijing 100044, China
P.O. Box 399, Beijing, China
Printed in the People's Republic of China

# Translator's Preface

HUNAN, this hinterland province larger than France, is essentially a region of hills and mountains apart from the plain around the Dongting Lake. It has a very ancient civilization. During the Warring States Period (403-221 BC) the kingdoms of Yue and Chu had their distinctive cultures here, and in subsequent centuries the central authorities found it hard to control its independence-loving people, owing to the difficulties of communication. Hunan has produced a great many talented writers. Outstanding among its twentieth-century authors are veteran woman novelist Ding Ling, Shen Congwen, and Zhou Libo who won fame after Liberation. Since the 80's a group of talented younger writers has emerged. One of them is Gu Hua, whose style is somewhat influenced by Shen Congwen.

In the thirties and forties Shen Congwen wrote brilliant idyllic stories and essays about west Hunan, conjuring up its countryside, folk customs and old way of life, to dispel the illusion that this was a "bandit area" shrouded in mystery. (see Panda Books "The Border Town and Other Stories" and "Recollections of West Hunan") Now Gu Hua is doing the same for south Hunan, a good example being his long story A Log Cabin Overgrown with Creepers (see "Chinese Literature" 1982, No. 12). However, his work has an added significance, as readers will see from *A Small Town Called Hibiscus.*

Gu Hua, whose real name is Luo Hongyu, was born in 1942 in a village of about a hundred households at the foot of the Wuling Mountains in south Hunan. His father, a small KMT functionary and accountant, died when Gu Hua was five, leaving his elder brother to support his mother and four younger children. Like other village boys, Gu Hua went barefoot, minded water-buffaloes, gathered firewood and carried charcoal to market. At the same time he attended the primary school in the little town of Jiahe.

Jiahe, so cut off in the past from the outside world that the local dialect is incomprehensible to people from elsewhere, was known as a centre of folk-songs, notably the cycle of songs to "accompany the bride" sung before a girl left home to get married. And Jiahe had an excellent middle school at which Gu Hua studied. Because he showed a flair for writing and won prizes for composition, he was put in charge of the blackboard bulletin; and if classmates failed to hand in contributions he would improvise poems to fill up the space. He read all the literature that he could lay his hands on, and longed to see something of the outside world. As his brother could only allow him one yuan a month as pocket-money, he failed to realize his dream of saving up fifteen yuan to hike to Chenzhou, the administrative centre 130 kilometres away.

After finishing junior middle school Gu Hua taught for a year in the Jiahe primary school. He then entered a technical school to study agriculture, after which he spent fourteen years, from 1962 to '75, in the Agricultural Research Institute in Qiaokou, formerly a waste land,

where he learned to grow rice, vegetables and fruit and
repair farm implements. There he married Yujuan, a
lively, pretty fellow worker. And there in the early
sixties he wrote his first short story.

In those days it was not easy for unknown writers to
get into print. Editors would first investigate their political record and class origin. However, after some of
the Party cadres in Chenzhou vouched for Gu Hua, his
first story *Sister Apricot* was published in 1962.

At Qiaokou, Gu Hua took part in the various political movements of that period, including the Four
Clean-ups Movement and the unprecedented "great
cultural revolution". He recalls, "Ingenuous and stupid,
I followed along blindly. I was criticized from time to
time, but never got into big trouble. However, I saw
my contemporaries, colleagues and friends playing different parts as they were tossed up or down by tempestuous movements, and that distressed and revolted me.
A few years ago I even felt that life was a kind of
Vanity Fair. . . ."

The heads of the Agricultural Research Institute encouraged Gu Hua's literary leanings and gave him time
off to indulge them. In 1970 he went for the first time
to a forestry station in the mountains to write. In 1975
he was transferred to the Chenzhou Song and Dance
Ensemble to give him more time for writing.

After the fall of the "gang of four" his dream of
travelling to broaden his horizons and see more of life
came true. In 1980 he became a member of the Chinese
Writers' Association, attended a writers' conference in
Beijing, went to lectures on literature and met many
well-known authors. In his spare time he wrote his
prizewinning *A Log Cabin Overgrown with Creepers,*

published in 1981, as well as other short stories. He resolved to write a novel about characters he knew in a small community which could mirror the turbulent age. Although he feared he was hardly up to this, he received encouragement from the editors of the Hunan People's Publishing House. And when the young writers taking the literary course were given a month off to do some writing, he went back to the forest in the Wuling Mountains and wrote a first draft of over 100,000 characters, which he tentatively entitled *A Remote Mountain Town*. In August he went back to Beijing to continue his studies, and in September handed in his incomplete manuscript. He expected it to be put on the shelf. Instead he was very soon told by the editors that they approved of it. They kept him in Beijing to revise and complete the novel. He was most impressed by the concern of these editors and older writers who encouraged him and made constructive suggestions.

It was Qin Chaoyang, an eminent literary critic, who changed the novel's title to *A Small Town Called Hibiscus*. And it was published in the monthly *Modern Times* (*Dangdai*) 1981, No. 1. It created a furore, for readers all over the country instantly related to it. To a great extent this was because it made a breakthrough in tackling a new theme. It is a devastating denunciation of the ultra-Left political line which prevailed in China from the late nineteen-fifties till the fall of the "gang of four". By presenting the ups and downs of seven or eight major characters in a small town in Hunan during this period, it shows us a microcosm of all China in those twenty stormy years. Gu Hua pulls no punches but writes forcefully with profound understanding based on first-hand experience. He exposes horrors, travesties of justice and the ultra-Leftists' denial of human kindness as well as other traditional Chinese virtues. At the same time he writes not with bitterness but with wry humour, which is how most Chinese who went through those terrible years tend to describe their experiences today. So this heart-rending novel also has many laughter-evoking scenes.

As early as '66, the first year of the "cultural revolution", Gu Hua in his remote agricultural research institute sensed "something rotten in the state of Denmark". Increasingly he grew more and more aware of the dangers of the ultra-Left line and the cult of the individual. To have voiced this at the time, of course, would have landed him in gaol. Then in 1979 the Third Plenary Session of the Party made a preliminary summing up of the Party's mistakes. The first genuine criticism of Leftism made by the Chinese Party, it marked a major historical turning-point, the start of a nationwide righting of wrongs and of condemning the cult of the individual. This reinforced Gu Hua's convictions and provided them with a theoretical framework. It also gave editors the courage to publish *Hibiscus*.

This novel has its detractors. A few local cadres complain that Gu Hua has treated them shabbily. Yet the record shows that grassroots cadres who resisted the lunacies of the ultra-Left line very quickly lost power and landed themselves — and their families — in serious trouble. Others object: Why make a positive character like Gu Yanshan, "the soldier from the north", an impotent drunkard? And would it not be more edifying, more effective in pointing out the dangers of ultra-Leftism, if the cadres who followed this line

were portrayed as impeccably moral instead of leading
loose lives like Li Guoxiang and Autumn Snake Wang?

I think such critics are still influenced by the idea
of a clear-cut distinction between "goodies" and "bad-
dies", black and white, which for so long was the bane
of Chinese writing. In this country too many stories,
plays and film-scripts have been written to formula,
describing stereotyped characters in stereotyped situa-
tions. How refreshing it is, then, when Gu Hua shows
us real flesh-and-blood human beings with weaknesses
as well as fine qualities. His characters are brilliantly
drawn and convincing.

In 1982, *Hibiscus* was one of six novels to receive
the first Mao Dun Literary Prize.

When Gu Hua heard that Panda Books intended to
publish *A Small Town Called Hibiscus*, he induced the
Cultural Bureau of Chenzhou to invite my husband
Yang Xianyi and me, as well as one of our editors, to
visit south Hunan for a week to absorb something of
the local atmosphere. It was a fascinating experience.
We visited a primeval forest in the mountains and
the forestry station below it where Gu Hua wrote most
of *Hibiscus* and where he gathered the material for
*A Log Cabin Overgrown with Creepers*. We discovered
that the little town Hibiscus is a composite of three
places. Its natural setting is Qiaokou, where a jade-
green river, East River, flows gently past the orchard
where Gu Hua sowed, grafted and pruned tangerine
trees at the foot of the Wuling Mountains majestic in
the distance beyond green foothills. The flagstone street
is based on Old Street in Jiahe, where Gu Hua went
to school and his family still lives. And the size of

Hibiscus at the start of the novel is approximately that of his childhood village.

As with the setting, so with the characters. Gu Hua does not write about real people in real life, as a number of Chinese writers tend to do, but invents characters on the basis of his observation of many individuals in different periods of recent Chinese history.

Gu Hua's output is impressive. By the end of 1981 he had to his credit two novels, four novellas, and over thirty short stories and essays, as well as songs. He is not a fast writer, however. He revises all his work four or five times, paying careful attention to technique and style.

A word now about this translation. An English translation is almost always longer than the Chinese original. As Gu Hua's narrative moves at a brisk pace, to convey this in English I have, with the author's permission, made certain abridgements, telescoped some passages, cut down on mixed metaphors which the Chinese delight in, or shortened lists of names or events such as the Three Anti or Five Anti Movements which would require footnotes or need to be paraphrased to make them intelligible to foreign readers. For instance, Gu Yanshan tells the children of Hibiscus stories about famous drunkards of old, listing six heroes and their exploits in their cups. I have retained one only, Wu Song who killed a tiger, who appears in the novel *Outlaws of the Marsh*.

Owing to the limitations of my English, now out of date after over forty years in China, I have failed to convey the raciness and earthiness of Gu Hua's language, which draws heavily on Chenzhou colloquialisms. I hope some younger sinologists will before long

12

make new translations to do justice to his graphic, pungent style.

Gu Hua says: What times we have lived through! There cannot be many countries whose writers have such a wealth of material at their disposal. He is planning to write another full-length novel about the years of turmoil.

*Gladys Yang*
*1982*

# Part 1
# A Small Town in the Hills
## (1963)

## The Local Customs

THE small town of Hibiscus lies in a valley bor-
dering the three provinces of Hunan, Guangdong
and Guangxi. From of old travelling merchants
have spent the night here, gallant men have gathered
here, and troops have contested this strategic outpost.
A stream and a river flow past it, converging about one
*li* away so that it seems like a narrow peninsula. South
of the ferry lies the way to Guangdong; west of the
stone arched bridge, the highway to Guangxi. In some
reign or other a local magistrate, wanting to display his
benevolence or to have his refinement recorded in the
district annals, had hibiscus trees planted along the
banks of the jade-green stream and river, to beautify
the place with flowers and green shade. He also sent la-
bourers to dig a lake in the marshland at the foot of
the back hill. Here lotuses were planted, fish were
raised, the lotus seeds and roots accruing to his
yamen. Whenever the lotus or hibiscus bloomed, this
plain in the Wuling ranges seemed rich and verdant.
The roots, trunks, flowers and bark of the hibiscus all
had medicinal value. The lotus, apart from yielding

seeds and roots, had big leaves as round as green gongs, on which dragonflies alighted, frogs poked up their heads, and dewdrops rolled. When picked, porters travelling some distance wrapped up rice and vegetables in these leaves; cakes could be steamed in them; they also served as covers for pedlars' loads or the bamboo basket of women going to market, or as hats for the boys minding buffaloes.... Hence the names Hibiscus River, Jade-leaf Stream and Hibiscus Town.

The main street of Hibiscus was not big. Paved with flagstones it was wedged between a dozen shops and a few scores of houses. These buildings were so packed together that if one shop stewed dog-meat, the aroma filled the whole street; if some child fell and knocked out a tooth or smashed a bowl, the whole street knew of it; neighbours often overheard the secrets girls confided to each other and the jokes between young married couples, then regaled the whole town with these titbits. If brothers fell out or husband and wife came to blows, the whole place was in a turmoil as all rushed to intercede. On days when there was no market, people fixed up long bamboo poles between their upstairs windows and those across the street, to sun their clothes and bedding. The wind blowing from the hills made these flutter like flags all the colours of the rainbow. And the clusters of red peppers, golden maize cobs, pale green calabashes and gourds hanging from the eaves formed bright borders on either side. Below, people came and went, cocks crowed, cats and dogs padded to and fro — it was a distinctive sight.

It was a neighbourly little town: at every festival the townsfolk treated each other to food and drinks. On the third of the third lunar month they made cakes;

on the eighth of the fourth month they steamed rice flour and meat; on the Double Fifth they prepared sticky rice dumplings and realgar-and-mugwort wine; on the Double Sixth some families had early fruit or vegetables; on the Double Seventh some had early rice; for the Mid-autumn Festival they made mooncakes; on the Double Ninth they picked persimmons; in the tenth month there were weddings; on the eighth of the twelfth month they made sweet rice porridge, and on the twenty-third saw the Kitchen God up to heaven. . . . Although the ingredients used by each household were much the same, clever young housewives introduced variations to give a distinctive flavour, and loved to have their cooking praised by the neighbours. Even on ordinary days, if some household had prepared fish, flesh or fowl, they were bound to give the neighbours' children a little, so that they would skip home to show it off to their parents. Later, their mothers would bring the children over to sit and chat for a while, as an expression of appreciation.

Though Hibiscus Town was so small, on market-days thousands of people gathered there. The main market was held on the flats by the river behind the town where a long pavilion stood, left from the old days. It had stone pillars, wooden beams and a black-tiled roof but no walls. Opposite it stood an old stage blotched with grease-paint. Just after Liberation, they kept up the old tradition of holding nine markets a month, on every day with a three, six or nine in it. From eighteen counties in three provinces came Han merchants, Yao hunters and physicians, and Zhuang pedlars. There were two markets for pigs and buffaloes, stalls of vegetables, fruit, mushrooms and edible fungus,

snakes and monkeys, sea-slugs, foreign cloth, daily ne-
cessities and snacks.... The place swarmed with people, rang with a hubbub of voices. If you looked down
from the back hill on fine days, you saw turbans, ker-
chiefs, straw hats; on wet days, coir capes and umbrellas
of cloth or oiled paper. The people seemed to be floating on a lake. Whether cold-water vendors or brokers
many of them made their living from these markets.
One poor fellow in the town was said to have built up
his fortune by collecting the dung from the two cattle
markets.

In 1958, the year of the Great Leap Forward, as everyone had to smelt steel and boost production, the district
and county governments restricted village markets and
criticized capitalist trends; so the Hibiscus markets were
reduced from one every three days to one a week, finally to one a fortnight. By the time markets disappeared,
it was said, they would have finished with socialism
and entered communism. But then Old Man Heaven
played up and they had bad harvests, on top of which
the imperialists, revisionists and counter-revolutionaries
made trouble. It wasn't so bad their failing to make
the great leap into communism; but instead they came
a great cropper, landing back in poverty with nothing
but vegetable soup in the communal canteen, and nothing
in the market but chaff, bracken-starch, the roots of
vines and the like. China and all her people developed
dropsy. Merchants stopped coming to the market, which
was given over to gambling and prostitution. Fighting,
stealing and kidnapping spread.... Then towards the
end of 1961 the county government sent down instructions to change the fortnightly market into one every
five days to facilitate trading. However, so much dam-

age had been done that Hibiscus market could no longer attract all those merchants from far away.

No longer was Hibiscus famed far and wide for its cattle markets, but Hu Yuyin's rice-beancurd stall did a flourishing business. Hu Yuyin was about twenty-five then. The customers who came to stand, sit or squat by her stall eating a bowl of beancurd were in the habit of calling her "Sister Hibiscus". Some jokers even called her "Hibiscus Fairy". Of course that was exaggerating, but she did attract attention with her black eyebrows, big eyes, face like a full moon, high breasts and graceful figure. According to Gu Yanshan, manager of the grain depot, "Sister Hibiscus's flesh is as white and tender as the beancurd she sells." She served customers cheerfully, affably and deftly, making no distinction between friends and strangers, between those smartly dressed and those in rags. She would see them off with a smile: "Another bowl? Like some soup to wash it down? Well, see you at the next market." Besides, her utensils were spotless, she served large portions and flavoured her beancurd well; so she did better business than other stall-holders. As she charged ten cents a bowl, with soup thrown in gratis, her stall was always thronged with customers.

"Do business with a smile, you'll make a pile." Yuyin had learned this from her parents. Her mother was said, as a lovely girl, to have been sold to a brothel, then to have run away with a young man to this border town. They changed their names, told no one where they came from, and opened a small inn which did good business. Not until they were in their forties and had importuned Buddha with incense, was their only child — Hu Yuyin — born to them.

In 1956, the year of the socialist transformation of capitalist enterprises, Yuyin and her young husband joined the Hibiscus farming co-op and became a peasant household. Only in the last couple of years had they started selling beancurd. At first Yuyin had taken a bamboo basket to market to peddle cakes of bran and wild herbs, later on cakes of sweet-potato flour. Then she set up her beancurd stall. This was not carrying on a family business; her miserable life had taught her to make a living out of it.

"Sister Hibiscus! Two bowls, please, with lashings of pepper!"

"Fine, I'll make it so hot that you get belly-ache!"

"Will you cure my belly-ache for me?"

"You silly ass!"

"A bowl of beancurd, missus, and a dram of spirits!"

"Here's a bowl with more soup to cool you off, comrade. You can buy liquor from that stall opposite."

"Sister Hibiscus, a bowl of your beancurd, white and soft as the palm of your hand. That'll see me home."

"Here you are. With a tongue like yours, your wife should make you kneel and tweak your big ears."

"I'd rather you tweaked them, sister."

"You lout, I hope my beancurd blisters your tongue. In your next life you'll be born dumb."

"Don't curse me. Don't want to lose an old customer, do you?"

Even when cursing someone, Yuyin smiled and her voice was music to his ears. She chatted and joked with her customers as if they belonged to the same family.

In fact some of these customers turned up each market-day.

First, Gu Yanshan, the manager of the grain depot. A bachelor in his forties, a northerner, he was an honest fellow. For some reason or other, the autumn before last he had suddenly notified Hu Yuyin that she could buy sixty pounds of rice seconds from his depot for each market. The young couple were so grateful for having their grain supply guaranteed that they nearly kowtowed to thank him. Each time Gu sat at her stall, silently watching the deft way Yuyin served her customers, he seemed to be admiring her youthful good looks. Because he was such a decent sort, however, this never gave rise to gossip.

Then there was Brother Mangeng, Party secretary of Hibiscus brigade. A demobbed soldier in his thirties, related to Yuyin's husband, he was her "adopted brother". His visit to her stall each market-day to eat two free bowls of beancurd implied that this was a legitimate business, and showed all who came to the market that it had the support of the Party secretary.

Another man who never paid for his beancurd was Wang Qiushe, Autumn Snake Wang, an activist in every political movement. He was in his thirties too, with a rotund face and ears, who normally looked like a laughing Buddha. But whenever the government sent a work team down to start some movement, he would run himself off his feet, blowing a whistle to summon the townsfolk to meetings, at which he would take the lead in shouting slogans. He took the night shift too to stand guard over bad characters. When the movement ended he seemed to shrink like a deflated balloon. A glutton for meat and fish, he spent three times as much as other people on food. Plumping himself down on the bench by the beancurd stall he would say brashly, "Two bowls, missus. Chalk it up." Sometimes, to her face, he would slap Yuyin's husband on the back, joking, "What's wrong, brother? Married all these years and still no bun in the oven. Do you need lessons from someone?" Husband and wife, flushed and angry, could not lose their temper with him. Although Yuyin disliked this cadger, she couldn't afford to offend him and so she always served him with a smile.

Another strange customer deserves special mention. This was Qin Shutian, known as Crazy Qin, one of the Five Categories* of bad characters. He had started off all right as a music teacher in a middle school and a director of the county's song and dance ensemble. But in 1957 he wrote a dance drama containing some folksongs which was declared reactionary, anti-Party, and so he was made a Rightist, dismissed from his job and sent home to work on the land. He stubbornly denied that he opposed the Party and socialism, simply admitting that he had made love to two women. He persuaded Party secretary Li Mangeng to change his "Rightist" label for that of "bad character". There was no end to his specious arguments. He came to Yuyin's stall when not too many people were about, cheerfully humming a line or two from some song.

"Crazy Qin! What devilish tune is that?" someone might ask.

"It's from the Guangdong dance *Up We Go*."

"Are you going up, a bad character like you? You're sinking lower and lower."

"Quite right. I've gone from bad to worse, must reform. . . ."

---

* Landlords, rich peasants, counter-revolutionaries, bad characters and Rightists.

In Yuyin's presence Qin was on his best behaviour. And because she felt that he had been unlucky, she often added extra oil and spice to his beancurd.

The traders who came to the market were a mixed lot. Apart from decent people there were hypocrites, opportunists, speculators, swindlers and vicious characters of every kind. But enough has been said about Yuyin's main customers for the time being. For some years, life in China has been like a market. So the characters in my story have no fixed roles but will simply take the stage in turn to perform for readers.

## The Manageress

Although so small, Hibiscus had three state-run shops: a department store, grocery and eating-house, one in the middle and one at each end of the flagstone street. They were thus in an excellent position to control all the town's commercial activities. The manageress of the eating-house, Li Guoxiang, newly transferred from the county's Bureau of Commerce, was particularly sensitive to the free market in Hibiscus. On market-days she kept a careful eye on the snack stalls, as these lured away so many of her potential customers. Like the old-style wife of a town head, she thrust out her small breasts to make a tour of inspection of the market, finally zeroing in on the beancurd stall. She was struck by the "Beancurd Beauty's" attraction for customers, quite apart from her good service and winning ways. "Confounded men!" she swore to herself. "They're like greedy cats prowling around that beancurd stall." Obviously Sister Hibiscus was her chief rival.

One market-day Li Guoxiang picked a quarrel with Sister Hibiscus. It started over a trifle. Yuyin's husband Li Guigui, the town butcher, had taken some finely shredded pork to the market. Fried with chilli it smelt most appetizing, and each bowl of beancurd was topped up with this — without any extra charge. So people were queueing up in front of the stall and some of them ate several bowlfuls, with the result that the state-run eating-house had very few customers. That would never do. Li Guoxiang hurried over to the stall and thrust out her left hand on which she sported a watch. "Show me your trading licence," she demanded.

At once Yuyin put down her ladle and said with a smile, "I pay the tax regularly to the tax-office after each market, elder sister. Everybody in town knows me. . . ."

"Your licence. Show me your licence! If you haven't one, I'll send my assistants to take over here."

Yuyin was taken aback. "Please don't, elder sister," she pleaded. "I'm selling a bit of beancurd, all open and aboveboard — not on the black market."

The people waiting for beancurd were provoked into taking her side.

"She has her stall, you have your eating-house. Why butt into her business? It's not as if she'd trampled anyone's grave."

"Don't poke your nose everywhere! Get away from here!"

"Why not clean up your own shop, get rid of all that rat shit in your noodles. Ha, ha. . . ."

Finally Manager Gu of the grain depot stepped forward to patch things up. "Forget it, we're all fellow

townsfolk. Just go and ask the town management committee and tax-office."

Li Guoxiang was furious. She wanted to denounce
them for encouraging capitalism. Hibiscus was a small
town but it had so many shady characters, all trying
to pull the wool over her eyes!

Li Guoxiang had worked in the personnel department of the county Bureau of Commerce. She was the
niece of Yang Min'gao, in charge of finance and trade
in the county committee, and she had won herself a
name in the criticism of capitalist trends in commerce.
It was said that in 1958 she had proposed that the
Bureau of Industry and Commerce should make a clean
sweep of all the stalls and pedlars in the county. Her
exploits had been reported in the provincial paper, and
she had become quite a personage. She very soon joined
the Party and was promoted. But nothing is ever plain
sailing. Just as she was about to be made a vice-commis-
sioner, word got out about her affair with an official
in the county committee, because when she went to hospital for an abortion she had to confess who had got
her in the family way. In order to protect such a promising young cadre, the matter was hushed up. Even
the doctor who had performed the abortion was suddenly transferred to Dongting Lake a thousand *li* away,
to take part in the drive to wipe out schistosomiasis.
And Li Guoxiang had to go down to Hibiscus to manage the eating-house — she hadn't even landed the job
of a section chief.

Li Guoxiang was thirty-two that year. A difficult
age for an unmarried woman who was unfit to be the
wife of a decent high official but who would not stoop
to marrying a man in a low station. But who could she

blame? Her whole youth had been a series of frustrated love affairs. At twenty-two when she joined the revolutionary ranks, she looked round for a suitable husband. Her first love was a platoon leader in the Military Service Bureau, who had one pip on his shoulder; but in those days girls used to recite:

One pip's too low,
Two leave me cold;
Three pips are best,
Four pips — too old.

So she quickly ditched that platoon leader and found a three-pip company commander who was not too old and had just divorced his wife in the countryside. However, he had a cheeky, bouncing boy who the first time he saw her called her "stepmother". That made her steer clear of the company commander. Her third love affair was also a flash in the pan. Then in 1956, when the Party called on its members to master science, she found herself a bespectacled intellectual in the Water Conservancy Bureau. They went steady for a year, until he was labelled a Rightist. Hell! What a close shave! She immediately broke with him. Now she was determined to find a section chief, even at the cost of becoming a stepmother. But this was easier said than done. Ten years had slipped away and with them her youth. Politically she was doing fine, but her chances of a good marriage were receding. Sometimes she felt quite desperate. First thing every morning she looked in the mirror, and while she did her hair her heart sank. Her eyes, once so big and bright, were dull now and blood-flecked, with dark circles under them and crow's-feet round them. Her cheeks, once rosy and dimpled, were sallow and flaccid. . . . Heavens, why should a girl deprived of love age so quickly? Now that she was unattractive, left on the shelf, how she envied women who were happily married.

If she were lawfully married, her illicit affair in the county town would be forgotten. Who didn't sow a few wild oats before marriage? On coming to Hibiscus this year she had sized up the Party members and cadres and discovered that the only eligible man was the northerner Gu Yanshan, the manager of the grain depot. A regular old bachelor, he had a bristly beard, dressed sloppily, and liked to drink. But someone in charge of the local bank divulged that Manager Gu's deposit was "over a thousand". Politically and financially he was up to par; too bad he was on the old side. Still, one couldn't have everything. And as the saying goes, "An old bridegroom dotes on his wife." Of course, it did occur to her how disgusting it would be to sleep with this swarthy fellow with his bristly beard — it would make her flesh creep. . . . But she was past her prime now, she must take action. She started to make up to Manager Gu, asking archly, "Old Gu, shall I get my cook to fry you a tasty dish to go with your liquor?" Or batting her eyelids at him she said, "Manager Gu, we've got a new consignment of spirits, and I've had two bottles put aside for you. . . ." "Aiya, your collar's so dirty! Shall I make another one for you?" Normally speaking, a man of his age should have been fired by such approaches; but this old bachelor was like damp wood, he didn't catch fire, didn't even smoke. How provoking! Li Guoxiang had to pocket her pride and give him a prod.

One evening the Party members of the supply co-operative and grain depot were summoned to a meeting. There was no electricity in Hibiscus then, and the meeting-place was lit by a sputtering paraffin lamp. The manageress ambushed herself in the dark at the foot of the stairs. As soon as Gu arrived she stepped up to him. "Not so fast, Old Gu! These stairs are as dark as a coffin. Can I take your hand?" He casually took her arm. Give Li Guoxiang an inch, she'd take an ell: she nestled up to him. He reeked of liquor, she of scent. But on the pitch-dark stairway no one could see them.

"Oh you've been drinking again? You reek of spirits," she giggled.

"What's come over you, clinging to me like a vine? Let go before someone comes." He was really as wooden-headed as a tree.

She pinched his arm, exclaiming, "How dumb you are! When a tasty morsel's offered to you, why not eat it?"

"You've brought your eggs to the wrong market," Gu retorted. "I understand spirits, but you're not to my taste!"

Heavens, what way was that to talk? How provoking! Luckily they'd reached the door of the meeting-hall. So, saying no more, both standing on their pride, they went and found their seats as if nothing had happened.

Fancy being snubbed by a bachelor in his forties! Li Guoxiang ground her teeth. Of course the waitresses in her eating-house had no idea what had happened, but they saw that her eyes were puffy the next morning, and she was in a foul temper. For no reason at all she stormed at one girl:

"Are you a tramp, coming to work in that short

skirt? Want to show off your plump white legs, do you? Disgusting! Are you apeing that beancurd pedlar? Shameless creature! Our state-run eating-house must set a good political example. Write a self-criticism for your Youth League secretary, analysing what made you doll yourself up like that!"

A few days later the manageress discovered why Old Gu had snubbed her. All because of that "Beancurd Beauty", Sister Hibiscus. Though she was a married woman, he supplied her at government expense with sixty pounds of rice seconds for each market! Calling them seconds was just his trick. They must be up to something on the sly. "Who are you, Hu Yuyin, and who am I? Yet you lord it over this small town!" She fumed over this for days, going so far as to gloat that Yuyin was childless. "What use are good looks if you can't have a baby!" She rather preened herself on her own two abortions.... Well, Gu Yanshan, Hu Yuyin, just you wait. Once I've dug in here, I shall show up your shameless carryings-on.

In her private life, Li Guoxiang often found herself stranded, but politically she forged full-sail ahead. Now that she had come down to Hibiscus, she decided to find the brigade's Party secretary and investigate the situation here, then make plans accordingly.


## Brother Mangeng and Sister Hibiscus

The banks of Hibiscus River had been planted with many hibiscus trees, said when old to turn into hibiscus spirits and take the form of bewitching girls to accost men passing by — one fine moonlight night someone had seen a troupe of them romping in the river, each with a handsome young man. Indeed, young men were drowned there every summer; so some foolish boys in the town both dreaded and loved the river, and the best swimmers among them hoped to meet the hibiscus fairies. The authorities wanted to build up the militia and, as this was endangered by such superstitious tales, they got schoolchildren to dig up the hibiscus and sow castor-oil seeds instead to provide lubrication oil for the air force.

The lake behind town had been planted with lotuses, but after communes were set up it was transformed into paddy fields. Still, a dozen or so big trees overgrown with creepers were left by the wharf; and it was a mystery how they had escaped being felled to smelt steel. Some said that hibiscus wood was not strong enough to make charcoal. Some insisted that these trees provided shade for passers-by. With the berries which covered the creepers like miniature bronze bells, they were reflected in the jade-green river and seemed to set its quiet water tinkling.

Brother Mangeng, the secretary of the brigade, had been demobilized in '56 and assigned to the district government, in the department of civil administration. Here by the ferry he had seen the only daughter of Innkeeper Hu. She had just finished washing a basket of clothes, and was leaning forward to watch the fish darting between the rocks. So when Mangeng came down the bank to wait for the ferry, the first thing he set eyes on was her lovely face reflected in the water. For a second he wondered if he had stumbled upon a hibiscus fairy. Which family could this beautiful girl belong to? He found her bewitching. Disregarding the tales about hibiscus fairies, he walked over, his eyes fixed on her enchanting reflection.

So two young faces appeared in the water bright as a mirror. The girl jumped with fright and flushed, dabbling one hand in the water to shiver the reflection, after which she sprang up and eyed him angrily. Then both stood there petrified, open-mouthed.

"Yuyin, how you've grown. . . ."

"Brother Mangeng, so you're back. . . ."

They had known each other as children. Mangeng, the son of the old ferryman, had gone up the hills with Yuyin in search of bamboo shoots, mushrooms and firewood. On opposite hills or cliffs they had serenaded or sworn at each other in fun. She might sing, "If you dare come here you'll get a surprise: with my sickle I'll kill you and gouge out your eyes." Little Mangeng would sing back, "Pretty girl over there, don't dare come to my side, or I'll veil you in red silk and carry you off as my bride." They sang a whole series of provocative songs, neither winning and neither losing. Yuyin swore, "You wretch! Who wants to be your bride? Pah!" Sometimes she wondered: Let's see if this lout really sends me a bridal sedan-chair. As they grew older and wiser and Mangeng joined the army, Yuyin would blush at the memory of those songs which made her pleasantly flustered, her heart beating fast.

The two young people were standing face to face on a stone slab, but both had lowered their heads to look at their shoes. Yuyin was wearing cloth shoes she had made herself, Mangeng, the gym-shoes issued him in the army. It was midday and very hot, cicadas were chirruping shrilly in the trees, and the ferryman on the other bank — Mangeng's dad — must be napping in the shade on some cool rock.

"Yuyin, your hands are as white as if you'd never done a stroke of work. . . ." Having broken the silence Mangeng looked down again. He could have kicked himself for his tactlessness.

"The idea! I work all day long. Don't wear a straw hat or carry a parasol, but somehow I don't tan. . . . If you don't believe me, look at my calluses." She spoke softly, as if to herself, but he heard each word.

She pouted, wanting to show him the palms of her hands; but she hesitated to stretch them out to him.

He smiled ruefully and reached out to feel her hands, but instantly drew back his own.

"Yuyin. . . ." He screwed up his courage to stare fixedly at her, a question in his wide eyes.

She knew intuitively what was in his mind.

"I'm in the clear . . . all on my own," she told him.

"Yuyin!" His voice faltered. He tensed and held out his arms.

"Don't you dare!" She fell back a step, her eyes brimming with tears like a little girl being bullied.

"All right, later. . . ." Mangeng calmed down, feeling as protective as an elder brother. "Better go home. Don't keep your folks on tenterhooks in the inn. Give them my best regards."

She picked up her basket, nodding. "Dad and mum are getting old and doddery. . . ."

"I'll come and see you one of these days, Yuyin." By now the ferryboat was crossing the river.

Yuyin nodded again, her chin touching her collar. Then she climbed the steps with her washing, looking back every three steps.

Mangeng went back to the district government grinning all over his face.

The district secretary Yang Min'gao was a local man and made a point of training local cadres. Of the score or so of youngsters in the district committee and district government, Li Mangeng was the one of whom he thought most highly. His class origin was good and so was his conduct; he was capable and ideologically sound. He had come back from the army with a good record, having won four merit citations in five years. Plans were afoot to abolish the district government and amalgamate different townships, and Yang was to work in the county in charge of finance and trade. He proposed to the county committee that young Li Mangeng should be made the head and Party secretary of Hibiscus — a large township in the hills. They had consulted Mangeng, and would soon confirm his appointment.

Yang's smart niece in the county Bureau of Commerce had just come to the district to investigate the supply and marketing work. Naturally she had all her meals in her uncle's hostel. And Secretary Yang, deliberately or by chance, always sent for Mangeng to join them. Mangeng had heard that this niece of Yang's was fast. She had chased men like a monkey picking corn-cobs, dropping one after another. So at the table he sized her up: Yes, she was smartly turned out. Before sitting down to eat she would take off her beige jacket of mercerized cotton, under which she wore only a collarless, sleeveless blouse revealing her plump white arms and neck in a highly suggestive way. Left and right under the cotton above her high breasts were what looked like two small buttons. Even Secretary Yang, normally so serious, would smile imperceptibly at the sight of his niece's plump white hands and the soft hollow of her throat. His niece had poise, having seen something of the world, and her expressive eyes kept sweeping over Mangeng as if to suck out his soul. He had never been subjected to such a searching scrutiny by a girl, and often flushed up to his ears. Then, feeling clumsy, he hung his head as if to count the legs of the stools and table.

After four meals together, they were addressing each other as "Little Li". The third day, after Secretary Yang had seen his niece off, he asked Mangeng with a smile, "Well, how about it? What do you think?" Mangeng was slow in the uptake. "Think about what, Secretary Yang?" he asked. It was really like playing a lute to an ox! How could a demobbed soldier in his mid-twenties be so dumb? They had just seen off a girl like a flower, yet this oaf asked her uncle what "How about it?" meant.

That evening, Secretary Yang had a serious talk with Mangeng, an act of condescension on his part for which any other young cadre would have shown appreciation. In his capacity as an uncle and a superior, he had mapped out in detail the young couple's family life and political future. Once again he asked, "How about it? What do you say?" To his surprise Mangeng stuttered, avoiding his eyes, before finally blurting out, "Thanks a lot for your concern, chief. Please give me a few days to think it over...." Yang glowered angrily, tempted to bellow, "Who do you think you are? A piddling cadre giving yourself such airs!"

Mangeng found a chance to go back to Hibiscus. Whether he and Yuyin met again to talk things over I have no means of knowing. But in those days it was the rule that all Party members and activists must get permission from their Party branch before they could get married. This was to ensure that Party members came from the right background, had no bad social connections and could be trusted. A few days later honest Mangeng respectfully reported his intentions to Secretary Yang.

"Congratulations, so you've fallen for the beauty of Hibiscus," drawled Yang Min'gao, lolling on a couch. After a good meal with drinks he was picking his teeth with a match.

"We knew each other as kids hunting together for bamboo shoots and mushrooms...." Mangeng's face was red.

"What's her class origin?"

"Small traders, I suppose. Like well-to-do middle peasants...."

"You suppose? What way is that for someone in civil administration to talk? What's the task of Communists?" Yang Min'gao sat up alertly, his eyes as bright as twenty-five-watt bulbs.

"Well, I...." Mangeng looked like a boy caught robbing an orchard.

"Representing the Party, Comrade Li Mangeng, I'll tell you: that innkeeper in Hibiscus was a gangster before Liberation. His wife's even more mixed, she was a prostitute. That's why her daughter's so seductive, see?" Yang Min'gao lolled back again on the couch. After working here all these years he knew the social connections and class origin of everyone in these parts.

Mangeng hung his head, close to tears.

"According to the Marriage Law, Little Li, you're free to choose your wife. But the Party has its rules too.

So make your choice: either keep your Party membership or marry the innkeeper's daughter."

Secretary Yang had stuck to principles. Naturally he
said not a word about his peach of a niece.

Army life had been simple; being demobbed was
complex. Like a tree blighted by frost, Mangeng lost
weight. Nor was that all. When the new town heads
were announced, his name was not on the list. He was
assigned as a cook to one township government.

Instead of going there to report for duty, Mangeng
went back to the ferryman's adobe cottage in Hibiscus
to help his ageing father. He had never risen high, so
this was not much of a fall. It was only right for a
boatman's son to be a boatman too. He knew the trade.

One fine moonlight night he met Yuyin again on the
wharf by the river. It was easier for them to meet now
that he was a ferryman.

"It's all my fault, Brother Mangeng. . . ." Yuyin
wept. Her pretty face reflected in the water was as
lovely as the full moon.

"Don't cry, Yuyin, you'll break my heart. . . ." An
ex-soldier like Mangeng could not cry, not even if
slashed with a knife.

"I know, Brother Mangeng. You had to choose between the Party and me. And I'm ill-fated. The year I
was thirteen a blind fortune-teller predicted that I'd
be the ruin of my husband — I haven't told anyone
this. . . ." She broke down and sobbed. In all her life
she had never hated anyone, never been hated. But
now she hated herself.

How could she be so superstitious seven years after
Liberation? But Mangeng hadn't the heart to remon-

strate. She was too pathetic, too frail, like the easily disturbed reflection of hibiscus in the water.

"Brother Mangeng, will you be my adopted brother? Take me as your younger sister, as we can't. . . ."

Her devotion would have melted iron. Mangeng, quite beside himself, threw his arms around her and kissed her on the mouth.

"Brother Mangeng, good brother, dear brother. . . ." She sobbed on his shoulder.

Her trust in him made him responsible for her. He released her, determined never to let her down. In that instant their relationship changed. The simple moral principles of the local people prevailed.

"From now on you'll be my dear younger sister, Yu-yin. . . . Though there's the river between us, we're living in the same town. As long as I live I swear to look after you."

That was a solemn vow.

When Li Guoxiang, manageress of the state-run eating-house, went to see the brigade secretary to ask about the class origin and conduct of Hu Yuyin, she found she had approached the wrong man. Not till she went down to the wharf did she realize that this was Li Mangeng whom she had met in the district government. To hell with it! She stopped in the act of stepping on to the ferry.

"Manageress Li! Where are you off to?" Confronting her was the "activist" Wang Qiushe who had just got off the boat.

Wang Qiushe was in his mid-thirties, sturdily built and neatly dressed. As she smiled at him politely it suddenly struck her: Why, of course, this "activist" must know all about Hu Yuyin — it should be easy to get it out of him.

So they walked off together and found out in the course of conversation that they had much in common, like two old friends reunited after a long separation.

## The Owner of the Stilt-House

This Wang Qiushe whom Li Guoxiang met at the ferry was quite a character. Originally a hired hand, he had ranked even lower than poor peasants, who belonged to the semi-proletariat. This made him a genuine proletarian. There was no tracing his ancestry as he had come here years ago as an orphan. So he had no relatives, no complex social connections. With this spotless record, pure as driven snow, he was fitted to soar to the sky or to go abroad. Unfortunately he couldn't pilot a plane or speak any foreign language — this was the fault of the old society. He had lived since boyhood in a tumbledown temple and acted as town-crier for five years. By the time of Land Reform he was twenty-two, glib and nimble, smart enough to run simple errands and ingratiate himself with the local bigwigs. Of course, they had sometimes cuffed him or kicked him for no reason; so at meetings to pour out past grievances he described himself as brought up on tears and bitterness, clouted on the head, trampled underfoot, so poor that in his late teens he still had no pants to wear, no rope to hang himself.

Thus he became a land-reform "activist". With his ready tongue he should have qualified to join the work team with a fountain-pen stuck in his tunic pocket. But just as he was going up in the world he came a sudden cropper over the tricky question of class stand: when sent to guard the property of a runaway landlord he shared the bed of the landlord's concubine. This was his way of proving that he had "stood up", for in the past he had never dared look such people in the face. Of course this was against the policy of the people's government and the rules of the work team. The concubine was punished for seducing a poor hired hand, while the "activist" lost his chance of joining the work team. If not for this, by now he might be riding in a jeep and working in the county government in charge of a million people. He had wept and snivelled to the work team, had slapped his face till his lips bled. Finally in view of his past sufferings, his hatred for the exploiters and his remorse, he was allowed to retain his hired-hand and "activist" status. He also received a first-class share of the fruits of victory: four sets of clothes, a whole set of bedding, two *mu* of irrigated land and — best of all — a stilt-house on the street paved with flag-stones.

This stilt-house, made entirely of wood, had been built by a despot landlord in the hills for his use when he came to markets and wanted to have it off with some prostitute. It was lavishly furnished. Only Wang Qiushe had forgotten to ask for farm tools and a water-buffalo. At first he was too happy to sleep for several nights, suspecting that this was a dream. His new wealth went to his head and instead of setting to work he started living it up, eating pork and drinking liquor at each meal, confident that he had enough to live on for years. With such good Party leadership, such an en-lightened people's government, China's prospects were so bright that, as the work team said, in eight or ten years they would have built socialism and advanced to communism. By then, food, clothes and housing would all be free, so why not take it easy? Each time he thought of that fine new society he turned somersaults on his grand red-lacquered bed, beside himself with joy.

But things had not turned out the way he had dreamed. All he had learned in the past was how to run errands, beat the gong and sweep the ground: he had no knowledge of farming. Good soil will not grow crops unless watered by its master's sweat. But planting out rice seedlings means wading through the muddy water, stooping. It is a back-breaking, blistering, sweaty business. He couldn't stand the dirt and the hard work. After a few years his fields were overgrown with weeds, overrun with mice and hares. Finally he quit farming, leaving his hoe and sickle to rust in a corner. On the sly he started selling his share of the land-reform fruits. When he went to restaurants and taverns, instead of throwing his money about he rationed himself so as to eke it out, but still he had some good binges and very soon put on weight. Sometimes the townsfolk saw no smoke above his stilt-house for weeks at a time, and wondered if he had learned the magic art of conjuring up a feast without even having to do the washing-up.

The proverb says, "Sit idle and eat, and your fortune will melt away." Muddling along like this, Wang Qiushe hadn't found himself a wife but had sold four-fifths of the furniture of the stilt-house, while his clothes were as ragged as before Land Reform. He lived on

credit or loans, indolent as an autumn snake* retreating
to its hole to hibernate. So in a few years he ate up his
property. Other land-reform activists had done so well
they had bought water-buffaloes, built themselves barns
and new houses, and fitted out their whole family with
new clothes. This made him green with envy. He longed
for another Land Reform, when he could get more
fruits of victory. "Hell! If I were running things, I'd
reclassify these buggers every year and have an annual
Land Reform to share out property!" Lying on his tattered matting in the stilt-house, his head pillowed on
his hands, he dreamed happily of whom he would label
a landlord, rich peasant, middle peasant and poor peasant. Who would be the chairman of the Peasants' Association? Dammit, he was the only man fit for that
post! Of course, he knew this was just wishful thinking.
Only once in a blue moon was there a redistribution of
property.

In 1954, some mutual-aid teams were set up in Hibiscus. He proposed joining one, pooling his land. But
no team would have him, well aware that he wouldn't
do a stroke of work, just ask for his share of the har-
vest. When agricultural co-operatives were set up, he
became a co-op member. Each co-op had a chairman,
several vice-chairmen, various production teams and
other organizations; and as they had to hold meetings
and pass on instructions, they needed someone politically reliable and articulate to run errands. This was
Wang Qiushe's chance — he was just the man for the
job.

Another of Wang Qiushe's distinguishing features

* Qiushe means "autumn snake".

was his readiness to help neighbour — all but the Five Categories of bad characters. If any family had a wedding or funeral he would go, uninvited, to help issue invitations, buy pork and liquor and prepare a feast. He spared no pains, not making outrageous demands but simply wanting to join in the fun and enjoy some good meals and snacks. At other times, if a pig or dog was killed, he offered his services to boil a cauldron of water, scrape off the bristles, clean out the guts, or shop for liquor or cigarettes. So imperceptibly he acquired the status of a "public servant".

Apart from doing people favours like this, he won the approval of the higher-ups. As he was a bachelor with so much space, whenever work teams came down from the county or district, most of them liked to stay with him. The floors of the stilt-house were dry, and with balconies in front and behind it was well ventilated. So Wang Qiushe got to know various district and county cadres, all of whom believed in class feeling. They saw that a polarization was taking place in the countryside, for here was Wang Qiushe still a poor hired hand after Land Reform, unable to afford a wife, with broken cooking utensils and tattered matting, bed curtain and quilts. So each year when the new crop was in the blade and the old one consumed, and relief grain had to be issued, the first recipient in Hibiscus was Wang Qiushe. Every two or three years he also received a set of padded clothes. It was as if the revolution had been made for the sake of men like Wang Qiushe — how could they be allowed to go hungry and cold in a socialist society? During the hard years after the Great Leap Forward, the county had been too poor to issue relief clothing. Wang Qiushe's padded clothes were in rags, with not a button left on them, and he made do by fastening them with a straw rope. In his view it would "disgrace the new society" if the government didn't give him relief. In winter, his lips were blue, his nose ran. Going to the commune headquarters he told the Party secretary:

"In 1959, chief, when the commune put on that class struggle exhibition, you took my old padded jacket, which was in better shape than this one I'm wearing. Could you unlock that room and let me swap them?"

The idea! Taking back a jacket from the class struggle exhibition, as if the present were worse than the past! The Party secretary felt this involved his class stand and class feelings, but as the government was still in no position to issue relief he took off his own padded jacket, not yet too shabby, and gave it to the "activist".

One of Wang Qiushe's favourite sayings was "the people's government feeds and clothes the people". And he showed his gratitude each time a work team came down to launch a new movement by summoning people to meetings, broadcasting through a megaphone, delivering documents, and standing guard at night. At meetings he took the lead in shouting slogans like a true activist. He did whatever the work team said. Political movements needed him and he needed political movements. They complemented each other.

Hu Yuyin's husband Li Guigui, the butcher, normally kept very quiet and couldn't be provoked. But dogs who don't bark may bite. He had summed up Wang Qiushe in a few derogatory lines which everyone recited:

The government has its quirks:
It trusts a slacker who shirks,

Ignores those who really work,
And those who do well it pulls up with a jerk.

Here I should explain why Wang Qiushe ate Yuyin's beancurd each market-day without paying. Among the victory fruits he had received had been a house next to Old Hu's inn. As the stilt-house was quite enough for a bachelor he didn't need this other house and had told Yuyin that he was willing to sell it to her for a couple of hundred yuan. That would cover the cost of all the beancurd he had eaten.

## "A Feast for the Mind" and
### *Wedding Songs*

Remember that expression "a feast for the mind"? This was bandied about in communal canteens in 1960 and 1961. For months at a stretch the commune members in the Wuling Mountains had no oil or meat and their vegetarian diet, so deficient in fat and protein, made their bellies stick to their spines. Of course this was blamed on the imperialists, revisionists, counter-revolutionaries and Old Man Heaven. Old Man Heaven had joined the Five Categories to sabotage the communal canteens. Later on the blame was also put on Peng De-huai, Liu Shaoqi and Deng Xiaoping, who were said to have opposed the Great Leap Forward and People's Communes. What was wrong with communal canteens? Every day they dished up a stew of greens and turnips without oil, to recall the bitter past — a far cry from life's sweetness today. "We're much better off than the Red Army on the Long March." What would they have thought of the communal canteens, those heroes who had eaten bark and roots and laid down their lives to liberate the Chinese people? These commune members in the hills could not understand abstruse theories: to them it was food that counted. All they knew was that their bellies were rumbling with hunger. The daytime was not too bad, but at night they couldn't sleep. So they devised a way to make up for their short rations by recalling the best meals they had ever had: whole chickens and fish, fat meat-balls and legs of pork. . . . What folk in the hills like best of course is dog flesh eaten on a snowy day. The appetizing smell makes neighbours' mouths water, and a bellyful of dog flesh keeps out the cold. It may sound too crude to be served at feasts, but there's nothing more nourishing. . . . Those recalling such meals and those listening to their accounts had a mental picture of those delicacies. They could almost smell them, and this set them drooling. Well, they'd have chances later to stuff themselves. Now that more than ten years had passed since Liberation and people had had some schooling, they fixed on the expression "a feast for the mind" to describe this type of reminiscing. The term did not remain in use very long. After all, what did the hard years amount to in China's long history, plagued by so many famines? Things had to be seen in the right perspective. New China had started from scratch twelve years ago and was still groping its way. The country and its people had to pay a price for learning how to live in a modern society. Leave it to posterity to decide which mattered most, their achievements or their shortcomings.

One spring night in 1963, Yuyin and her husband Li Guigui held a different kind of "feast for the mind" in the inn. A loving couple, married for seven years, they still had no children. Li Guigui was the elder by four years, and, although a butcher by trade, was notoriously timid. If he met a fierce-looking water-buffalo or dog in the road he would tremble and step aside. Someone quipped, "Guigui, why aren't you afraid of pigs?"

"Pigs are too stupid to bite and they don't have horns. All they can do is grunt!" Guigui didn't mind being teased for cowardice. What hurt him was when well-meaning or malicious people laughed at him for failing to father a son, saying his capable wife was only an empty flower-vase. Unknown to anyone, including her, he had fortified himself by eating kidney and gristle. Sometimes, unable to sleep at night, he held back his sighs for fear of upsetting Yuyin.

"If only we had a son, Yuyin, or even a daughter."

"Yes, twenty-six I am now. It's worrying."

"If you have a baby you can leave the housework to me. I'll wash the nappies and put it to sleep at night."

"Will you suckle it too?" Yuyin giggled.

"No, I haven't your two meat dumplings on my chest."

"Get away with you!"

"Every evening I'll cuddle that baby and croon it to sleep. Every day I'll smother its little face with kisses."

"Shut up!"

"Why, have I said anything wrong?"

"You're going crazy wanting a baby. It's cruel to tease me about it." Yuyin wept.

Guigui hadn't realized that a childless woman always thinks of herself as a hen that can't lay eggs.

"There, there, Yuyin, why cry? It's not your fault. Crying's bad for your eyes. Look, your pillow-case is wet." Guigui tried to comfort her. "Even if we never have kids I won't hold it against you. Just the two of us, only two mouths to feed, working in the team and trading a bit on the side, we're living as well as anyone in town. When we're old we'll look after each other. Want me to swear it?"

Yuyin thought that would bring bad luck. She hastily stopped crying and sat up to cover his mouth. "You wretch!" she scolded. "Want me to slap you? Can't you talk about something else? If I let you down by not having a baby you may not blame me, but people talk behind my back in the market."

The winter after Li Mangeng had explained why he couldn't marry her, Yuyin had married Li Guigui and given all her affection to her husband. She believed she was born under a lucky star but might bring bad luck to him, so considered him more precious than her own life.

The evening before a market they always stayed up late to grind rice, fetch water from the river, then boil the beancurd and put it in a big vat. They stood for four or five hours, one on each side of the mill, turning it round, and Yuyin carefully fed the millstone with handfuls of rice steeped in limewash. Face to face, looking into each other's eyes, they chatted about whatever came into their heads. Instead of crying now, Yuyin said teasingly:

"It's not always the woman's fault if there's no baby."

"Heaven knows, we're both of us fit and strong." Guigui was not going to admit that it might be his fault.

"I heard the schoolmistress say they give check-ups now in the hospital for men as well as women." Yuyin reddened as she watched for her husband's reaction.

"What check-up? You can have one. I'm not making a fool of myself!" Guigui's face was as red as a ripe persimmon.

"I just mentioned it, I haven't asked you to go, so don't fly off the handle." They both knew it was only natural to have children, but even if they remained childless they must keep their self-respect. Sometimes when she felt desperate, Yuyin would stare at her husband, tempted to say:

"Which means more to you, an heir or my good name? Maybe Wang Qiushe of the stilt-house wasn't just joking when he said you should get someone else to try. . . . Heavens, what a nonsensical notion!"

Guigui seemed to know what she was thinking. He glowered at her. "Don't you dare! I'd break your legs!" Of course neither voiced these ideas, but their eyes gave them away. The people of that small hill town might not be rich, but what they prized most in life was a good reputation, and they had feudal ideas about chastity.

As time went by and still she did not conceive, Yuyin, whose only schooling had been in the class to wipe out illiteracy, decided that it was because she and Guigui were ill-matched. The year that she was thirteen, that blind fortune-teller had foretold from her horoscope that she would be lucky in life but would not bear a child and would be the death of her husband, unless she found a man born in the year of the Dragon or Tiger, whose trade was butchering. Then they would be happily married and have children. Because of this, after she was fifteen her parents searched for four years for a suitable man willing to come to live in the inn. Unable to find one, they stretched a point and chose Li Guigui. He was at least a butcher, good-looking and strong.

However, being born in the year of the Rat he was timid and blushed at the sight of a girl. Still he was honest and wouldn't get out of hand. They had to settle for Guigui. But when the young couple married, although the wedding was lively — on a grander scale than ever before in Hibiscus — it hadn't brought them good luck.

It was in 1956, when the county's song and dance ensemble had come like a troop of fairies to the Wuling Mountains to collect material. They were headed by their director Qin Shutian, now known as Crazy Qin. These pretty girls who could dance and sing won the hearts of all in Hibiscus. In those parts, before Liberation, the women all danced and sang their traditional *Wedding Songs*. No matter how rich or poor a family, before a girl's marriage other young women came to her home to sing and dance. There were a hundred or so of these songs ranging from "Seeing Off Sister" to "Greeting Sister-in-law", "Persuading Mother", "Cursing the Go-between", "The Hateful Bridegroom" and "The Chair-bearers' Song". Some described the bride's grief at leaving home and her dread of marriage, others attacked feudal conventions and arranged marriages. Thus "The Hateful Bridegroom" went:

> A bride of eighteen, a bridegroom of three,
> Who wet the bed each night;
> He was shorter than his pillow,
> Not up to a broom in height.
> At midnight when he bawled to be fed,
> "I'm your bride, not your mum!" she said.

The melodies were also very varied. Some had the simplicity and verve of folk-songs, some the gentle lilt of lullabies. The merry tunes conjured up flowers and tinkling brooks; the sad ones breathed resentment; the defiant ones were rousing. All alike were redolent of the Wuling Mountains.

Qin Shutian came from Hibiscus, where his father had taught in the school. He had brought his actresses here to compile *Wedding Songs*, intending to make its main theme opposition to feudalism. He and the township secretary persuaded Hu Yuyin's parents to let him put on his production at her wedding. Although her mother was old, she had learned to sing as a girl and had taught her daughter, who knew the whole of *Wedding Songs* by heart. With her good looks, sweet voice and expressive acting she was one of the finest singers in Hibiscus. Indeed, Qin Shutian and his actresses thought it a pity that such a girl should marry while still in her teens.

That evening the inn was brightly lit and richly decorated for the wedding and the performance. The actresses and Yuyin had made up, and other young women sat round them to join in the singing.

> Blue skirt, red scarf, the girl has grown;
> The bridal sedan-chair breaks her heart.
> A toss of a stone and the birds have flown,
> Two sweethearts are torn apart.
> Forbidden to make her his wife,
> He will love her all his life.
>
> We sing of girls who must part,
> Our sister is going away;
> Tomorrow she will be gone,
> Let us sing together today.

> They are marrying off their daughter,
> Throwing her out like water. . . .

Amid singing, dancing and weeping, Yuyin sang and wept too. For grief? For joy? She felt as if in a dream, confused by the bright, dazzling colours. The actresses, lovely as fairies, danced around her. . . . Perhaps it was because Qin Shutian, to stress opposition to feudal ways, had cut out some of the merry songs in the original, that the tone of the whole performance was tragic and resentful. Li Guigui the bridegroom was rather disappointed, while the young couple's parents were afraid that this would spoil their luck. This must have dawned on Qin Shutian, for to conclude the performance he led them all in singing *The East Is Red* and *The Sky in the Liberated Areas Is Bright*. So finally light triumphed over darkness.

Before long, Qin Shutian took his ensemble back to town and produced a full-length dance drama on the basis of this material from Hibiscus. It was successfully staged in the county town and the provincial capital, and he published an article in the provincial paper on scrapping feudal customs and evolving new ones. So while still under thirty he made himself a name and won a prize. But the tide soon turned against him. The next year in the anti-Rightist campaign his dance drama was condemned as an attack on the new society on the pretext of opposing feudal customs. How outrageous, how vicious and reactionary to use the socialist stage to vent his hatred of socialism! Qin Shutian was made a Rightist, dismissed from his post and sent back to Hibiscus to be reformed through labour. After that he appeared each market-day to sell the straw sandals he had made or to pick up cigarette stubs. Everyone called him Crazy Qin.

Although Yuyin and Guigui were not in trouble, they felt ashamed of their part in the business. What was feudal about the new society? Why oppose feudalism? By lumping feudalism together with the new society Qin Shutian had committed a crime and landed himself in the Five Categories. Because of Yuyin's involvement her luck had been spoiled and so all these years after marriage she was childless.

## Crazy Qin

On one partition of the public lavatory behind the state-run eating-house in Hibiscus there appeared a counter-revolutionary slogan. Two security men from the county came down to handle the case, and put up in Wang Qiushe's stilt-house. Because Wang was poor, politically reliable and good at running errands, they naturally relied on him to help them. What the slogan was, only Manageress Li Guoxiang and the two security men knew. And they weren't telling — that would have been counter-revolutionary propaganda. Wang Qiushe had some idea, but could not disclose a secret connected with the people's government. The townsfolk felt uneasy, suspecting each other.

Li Guoxiang and Wang Qiushe told the security men that although Hibiscus was small, on market-days many shady characters flocked there. And Hibiscus itself had over twenty landlords, rich peasants, counter-revolutionaries, bad elements and Rightists; in addition to many people with bad family backgrounds and social connections. Before Liberation the townsfolk had drunk, whored and gambled. Few of them had a clean record. Even the government cadres, Party and Youth League members rubbed shoulders with these people all the time or were related by marriage, so that class distinctions were blurred.

The security men made a careful class analysis of Hibiscus. Then, following their usual practice in such cases, they, Li Guoxiang and Wang Qiushe sent for all the Five Categories. These people were under the surveillance of Li Mangeng, Party secretary of the brigade, who used to give them a lecture every so often. He had assigned Crazy Qin the job of fetching the others, lining them up and counting heads on such occasions.

Crazy Qin, now over thirty, was content with his lot. His family origin was not too bad and he was a distant relative of Li Mangeng, whom he had persuaded to change his label from "Rightist" to "bad element". He claimed he had never opposed the Party or people, but had made love to two actresses — this had not come out in the anti-Rightist campaign — so the label "bad element" was more appropriate. Li Mangeng agreed and announced this at a mass meeting. And soon, because Qin was well educated, wrote fine calligraphy and was a good organizer, he put him in charge of the Five Categories.

Crazy Qin facilitated Li Mangeng's job of "supervising and remoulding" them. Each time they were summoned for a dressing-down, Li had only to call "Crazy Qin!" and he would answer in a ringing voice "Here!" race over like a sports master, stand smartly to attention and salute. "Report! The bad element Qin

Shutian is present!" He would then lower his head submissively. At first Li and the other cadres had found this performance amusing; later they took it for granted.

"Listen to me, Crazy Qin. After supper all the Five Categories are to fall in in front of brigade headquarters."

"Very good! I'll see to it." Wheeling round Qin dashed off again like a sports master. And that evening he would muster all the Five Categories punctually in front of the brigade office, line them up, call the roll and then report the number ready for inspection.

Qin Shutian had his own way of running these people. He told different individuals:

"We're all on the blacklist, but some of us are blacker than others. For instance you're an ex-landlord, who grew fat off the peasants before Liberation; you're the worst. You're a rich peasant, who did some work yourself but exploited others through usury, trying to climb up to be a landlord; you're second worst. As for a counter-revolutionary like you, who treated the people as your enemy, your category is the most dangerous. Mind you watch your step."

"And you? What do you count as?" they might retort.

"Me? I'm a bad element. That's more complicated, as there are different kinds: thieves, rapists, swindlers, hooligans, kidnappers, men who run gambling dens. Generally speaking, their family background's not bad. Of all the Five Categories, this is the best. We shall go to different hells after we die."

While stressing his superiority to the rest, he never said a word about Rightists, how they opposed the Party and socialism, or to which hell they would go.

Qin Shutian had taught music in a middle school besides directing the song and dance ensemble, so he could play various instruments and sing, could write, paint and play chess, and put on a good performance in the lion dance. He was for ever humming or singing. During the hard years class struggle slackened down, and when families round about married off their daughters he was invited to play in the band and to sit down to the feast alongside poor peasants. So the townsfolk regarded him differently from other members of the Five Categories. Besides, he was allowed to atone for his crimes by writing up most of the slogans for different movements.

The previous spring, maybe to show that he had remoulded himself, Qin had used his flair for music to compose a *Song of the Five Categories*.

> The Five Categories, diehard reprobates,
> Oppose the Party, people and the state;
> But our militiamen are on the spot,
> Whoever stirs up trouble will be shot.
> Come clean! Confess! There's no hiding,
> It's best to be law-abiding.

He prided himself on this song and asked permission to teach it at the next meeting to harangue the Five Categories. But they were too pig-headed to learn, and with a smile Party Secretary Li stopped him. Later on, however, all the children learned it and sang it everywhere, so that it had some social influence.

Opinions varied about Crazy Qin. Some commune members admired him as a scholar who knew about everything under the sun and could explain matters from a Marxist, historical-materialist standpoint. Some thought he was only making a pretence of being honest and enthusiastic. Others couldn't understand why he was always so cheerful. Yet others said it was only in the daytime that he smiled and sang; in the evenings in his hut he sobbed his heart out. Militiamen standing guard by Hibiscus River often saw him walking up and down the bank — did he want to drown himself? Not likely. He was probably thinking over his past and future. . . .

At all events no one disliked Crazy Qin, and this went for Sister Hibiscus, who sold beancurd, as well as Gu Yanshan, manager of the grain depot. On market-days they greeted him with a smile. And out in the fields people liked to sit with him in the shade and get him to sing to them or tell them a story. Young wives and children were not afraid of him either, but would give him various errands or odd jobs to do. Some children lacking in class consciousness even called him "Crazy Uncle Qin".

Crazy Qin led the brigade's twenty-two bad characters, all with lowered heads, to a downstairs room reeking of pickles in the state-run eating-house. When they had found bricks to sit on, Manageress Li Guo-xiang and activist Wang Qiushe brought in the security men. The latter called the roll, and each bad character in turn had to stand up to be inspected. There was no deceiving these stern, sharp-eyed security men. When they called the name of an old counter-revolutionary, a boy of eleven or twelve piped up, "Here." That struck them as strange. How could this child born after Liber-ation be a pre-Liberation counter-revolutionary? Crazy

Qin hastily reported that the boy's grandad was ill in bed, coughing blood, so his grandson had come in his place to pass on to him any instructions from above.

Wang Qiushe spat at the boy. "Stand in the corner! So the blasted Five Categories are raising successors! The class struggle will have to go on for generations!"

Now Li Guoxiang produced a stack of white paper, gave one sheet to each delinquent and ordered them to write the slogan: "Long live the Three Red Banners: the Great Leap Forward, the General Line and the People's Communes!" They must write it twice, first with the right hand, then with the left. They guessed that this was to compare their writing with that on some reactionary slogan. The bolder of them took this in their stride, knowing that whenever a case like this cropped up the security men would investigate them first. The more timid of them were shaking in their shoes.

To the great disappointment of the security men and Li Guoxiang, ten of these Five Categories elements couldn't write, and vouched for each other that this was the case. Wang Qiushe explained, "The bigger landlords in these parts all lit out to Hong Kong or Taiwan before Liberation, just leaving this riff-raff here."

Qin Shutian, using first his right hand then his left, was the only one to fill two sheets of paper with big, neatly written characters; though the security men could have seen plenty of his writing in the slogans in the street or on rocks. When all these suspects able to write had written out the slogan, they were warned that they must abide by the law, then dismissed.

Crazy Qin was the Number One suspect. But the brigade cadres reported that he had worked hard these last few years and made no trouble. Besides, his writing didn't match. Then Li Guoxiang and Wang Qiushe pointed out that Hu Yuyin who sold beancurd had a bad family background, an ex-gangster father, an ex-prostitute mother; and she was a tramp, making up to cadres to corrupt them. So on the next market-day the security men went to her stall to eat beancurd, and sat there quite a while to size up the situation. They saw that the pretty stall-holder served customers with a smile, far more politely than the women attendants in most state-run restaurants. And she didn't know enough characters to write a slogan. Besides, she was doing so well with this side-line of hers, why should she hate and curse the Three Red Banners?

Then Li Guoxiang suggested that in the absence of other clues they should make all the townsfolk who could write set down their understanding of the Three Red Banners. But again that got them nowhere.

That slogan written up in the lavatory behind the eating-house had unsettled and alarmed everyone in Hibiscus. Everyone came under suspicion. In the end this counter-revolutionary case remained unsolved but it left the town under a cloud.

Although the case had not been solved, Wang Qiushe was made an assistant of the Public Security Bureau, with a salary of twelve yuan a month. And Li Guo-xiang gained in prestige, becoming a rival to Gu Yan-shan, manager of the grain depot. She liked to strut up and down the flagstone street, pausing at each door to ask:

"Got a visitor? Go and register with Security Officer Wang. You must say when he arrived and when he's leaving, what his class is, his relationship to you, and whether he has a letter from his commune or brigade. . . ."

"When did you put up this couplet on your door? The characters 'People's Commune' are practically washed out. And how can you hang a cape under Chairman Mao's portrait?"

"Say, grandad, how much do you think that woman makes selling beancurd each market-day? Is it true that her husband's bought bricks and tiles and means to build a new house?"

"Doesn't the Rightist Qin Shutian live next door? You must keep an eye on him, watch who visits him. Security Officer Wang will tell you what to do. . . ."

The manageress spoke politely, as if with friendly concern, but she left people feeling nervous and put out. As time went by, if she appeared in the street they exchanged warning glances and held their tongues. Even dogs and cats made themselves scarce. It was as if everyone's fate was in her hands. Hibiscus had been quiet and law-abiding, all the townsfolk on good terms; but now they began to sense that this newly arrived manageress of the eating-house had eclipsed Gu Yanshan, to whom they had looked for guidance, and that there was trouble in store.


## The Soldier from the North

Gu Yanshan, in an old sheepskin jacket, had come south with the army thirteen years ago and stayed to work in Hibiscus. He had modified his northern accent so that the local people could understand him, and accustomed himself to eating paprika, snake, catflesh and dogflesh. Tall and sturdily built with a shaggy beard, bulging eyes and ferocious features, he looked rather intimidating. When he first arrived and stood in the street, arms akimbo, the children fled in terror. And their mothers to frighten them at night would say, "Don't cry! That bearded soldier will catch you!" Actually, he was neither fierce nor hot-tempered. When the townsfolk knew him better they said, "Old Gu looks like a devil but has a heart of gold."

He had married shortly after Liberation, a plump girl from the north with a glossy pigtail. But in less than a fortnight she had left, pouting and tearful, and she had never come back. No one had heard them squabble; but this made Old Gu lose face badly. He didn't blame the girl, it was his own fault. Feeling guilty of having tricked her into the marriage, for several months he would look no one in the face; and the townsfolk, not knowing the truth, thought he had lost some important document. The fact was that in the guerrilla fighting and tunnel warfare up north he had received a thigh wound which left him impotent. Few men will admit to such a thing for fear of making people hoot with laughter. Besides, in those days, with bullets whistling round your ears and explosions smothering you with dust, waking at night you'd feel to see if you were still in one piece. Risking his neck in the War of Liberation, he could drag on for a few years. Didn't other wounded men grit their teeth to soldier on? Even with bullets and shrapnel embedded in them. If he could stick it out till victory, then live a peaceful life, it shouldn't be difficult, surely, to clear up this trouble.

However, his company's political instructor, who was rough and ready but as concerned for each of his fighters as an elder brother, discovered on the march what pain this platoon leader getting on for thirty was in. So when they reached Hibiscus, he left him to work in that salubrious district. Still Gu was ashamed to go and see a doctor. Instead he dosed himself — uselessly — with herbal medicine. This fighter who had joined in overthrowing feudalism still had many feudal ideas and no faith in science. To him it would have been too humiliating to let white-coated doctors in gauze masks poke and prod him and examine him as if inspecting a horse. Later he heard that once a man took a wife, this illness of his would clear up. Having weighed the pros and cons, he decided not to marry a local girl but one from his old home, because then if it didn't work out and she left him, that wouldn't make a bad impression in Hibiscus. In a sense he had played safe, but the outcome was disastrous. Because he had rejected science, science had not come to his rescue; and to clear his conscience he now sent that girl a monthly allowance.

It was some time before they realized in Hibiscus that Manager Gu must have some unmentionable illness, which not even the best of women could tolerate. Well-meaning, foolish go-betweens proposed various matches to him, but he turned them all down. So gradually they gave up approaching him. This was why he had snubbed the advances of the manageress of the state-run eating-house, to whom no one had explained the situation.

However, Old Gu though childless had plenty of friends. Over half the Hibiscus children called him "Dad", and he was so fond of them that his place was always full of romping girls and boys rolling on the bed.

His table and floor were piled with picture-story books, lollipops, toy cars, aeroplanes, tanks and guns. He paid some children's school fees, bought pencils and rulers for them. Some of the town's economists estimated that he spent over ten per cent of his pay on these "adopted" sons and daughters. Whenever a young couple married, he was always invited to the feast and would make a few well-chosen remarks, besides giving them a present neither too large nor too small. People were in the habit, too, of inviting him to a good meal they had prepared for some elderly or important visitor. They would introduce him as "Manager Gu, an old revolutionary from the north" as if this reflected credit on their household.

As time went by, Old Gu's presence in Hibiscus had a stabilizing effect. If neighbours quarrelled over relative trifles, one would say, "Come on, let's ask Old Gu to decide. See if he doesn't bawl you out."

"Does your family have a monopoly of Old Gu? He belongs to all Hibiscus! If he says I'm in the wrong, I'll take his word for it."

And Old Gu with his bulging eyes, shaggy beard and intimidating look loved to settle their disputes by rebuking or reasoning with them. He tried to solve all contradictions. If money was involved, he might dip into his own purse. So often both parties to the dispute would come together to apologize and thank him. If he happened to go to the county on some business for a few days, every evening when folk took their rice bowls out to the flagstone street to have their supper they would ask each other:

"Seen anything of Old Gu?"

"Why isn't he back yet?"

"He's not going to be promoted or transferred, is he?"

"We should all send a petition to the county: If he's to be made an official, why not here?"

It is still a mystery why Old Gu offered to let Sister Hibiscus buy sixty pounds of rice seconds for her bean-curd stall for each market. This later landed him in serious trouble, but he never would admit that he had done wrong. Nor did his attitude to her change even after she was classified as the widow of a rich peasant. But this is anticipating.

In 1963, the County Bureau of Commerce sent the men in charge of the Hibiscus markets the following directive, with a bright red chop on it:

These last few years in your town, pedlars taking advantage of the state's financial difficulties have engaged in speculation and profiteering. Quite a few commune members have given up farming for trading, using state materials to prepare various snacks, disrupting commerce and sabotaging the collective economy of the people's communes. Please check up on all the stall-holders in Hibiscus and close down all illegal stalls. Report the results of this clean-up to the county.

To this was appended a comment "Approved" from the Finance and Trade Section of the County Commit-tee. And Secretary Yang Min'gao had added: "Atten-tion must be paid to these problems." Clearly those in authority supported this directive.

This document was delivered to Gu Yanshan. As

Hibiscus had no Market Control Committee, other cadres headed by Old Gu were responsible for running things, settling disputes and issuing trading licences. Gu called a meeting of the head of the tax-office, the managers of the supply and marketing co-operative and the credit co-operative, and Hibiscus Brigade Party secretary Li Mangeng. The tax-officer suggested co-opting the manageress of the state-run eating-house, since she had recently shown such an interest in market control and public security. But Old Gu said there was no need to trouble her, as her eating-house came under the supply and marketing co-op, the manager of which was present.

First Gu read out the document. Then they started discussing it and speculating:

"Obviously someone here has lodged a complaint!"

"People have to eat, even small pedlars."

"Cadres in government pay, eating state grain, don't seem to care whether the people have oil, salt, firewood and rice or whether they go hungry!"

"That 'counter-revolutionary slogan' set Hibiscus by the ears. This is going to turn things even more upside-down."

Li Mangeng, the only one to hold his tongue, knew that Li Guoxiang was behind this. He had witnessed her fracas with Yuyin. And she was the smart niece of Yang Min'gao whom he had met some years before in the district. She appeared much older now, sallow and wrinkled, so that at first he hadn't recognized her. Apparently still a spinster, she was devoting all her energies to the revolution. A few days previously she and Wang Qiushe, with two security men, had lectured the Five Categories and checked on their handwriting;

so she wasn't simply running the eating-house. Moreover Wang Qiushe had been appointed a security officer without anyone consulting the Party secretary of the brigade. And now here was this directive from the County Bureau of Commerce — odder and odder! As to what Li Guoxiang's aim was, he didn't give that much thought. Indeed, none of them analysed this carefully.

Finally they concluded that in view of the policy of encouraging trading in the countryside, it would not be right to close down all stalls, they should have a legitimate status. They made the tax officer responsible for re-registering all the pedlars in Hibiscus and issuing temporary trading licences. He should then write a report on the action taken and the policy he had followed, and send this to the County Bureau of Commerce to be passed on to Secretary Yang Min'gao.

The tax-officer asked Li Mangeng with a smile, "Sister Hibiscus who sells beancurd is your adopted sister, isn't she? Does your brigade approve of her keeping that stall?"

"Never mind whether she's my sister or not," said Mangeng. "Official business must be done according to official principles. Has Yuyin paid her tax each market-day? She's paid our brigade for the days she's not come to work. Normally she and her husband work hard for the collective. We consider her stall as a family side-line in keeping with the Party policy, so we think she should have a licence."

Old Gu nodded his approval.

When the meeting broke up, the two of them stayed on there, having something on their minds.

"Smell anything fishy, brother?" Old Gu might be easy-going, but he was shrewd.

"Manager Gu, a hornet has broken into our hive. We shan't be left in peace," was Mangeng's answer.

"Well, let's just hope there's no trouble. . . ." Old Gu sighed. "But one rat turd can spoil a pan of soup."

"All the townsfolk are behind you, and you're the only one who can handle this so that Sister Yuyin and the rest don't land in trouble."

"Yes, she's in a weak position. But so long as we have the say, we can see that no harm comes to them. . . . In a couple of days I'll go to town to look up some old comrades-in-arms, to figure out a way to get this hornet transferred. . . ."

Having exchanged views they went their different ways.

That autumn the manageress of the state eating-house was transferred back to the county, to be a section chief in the Bureau of Commerce. Then the Hibiscus townsfolk breathed more freely, as if the dark cloud hanging over them had been wafted away.

Little did they know that one night while they were snoring peacefully in their beds, a hand-written report from the County Security Bureau was lying on the desk of County Party Secretary Yang Min'gao. The only light in his office was a table-lamp on his desk. Yang, seated in a wicker chair, was studying this report about a reactionary "clique" in Hibiscus. On a sheet of official stationery he drew a diagram, putting question-marks against the name of Gu Yanshan, the "soldier from the north". He was in two minds about him. The diagram of this "clique" was as follows:

```
┌──────────── The Beancurd Beauty ────────────┐
│        (one of the new bourgeoisie, daughter of      │
│              a gangster and a prostitute)            │
│                                                      │
│ Li Mangeng                              Gu Yanshan   │
│ (brigade secretary with          (manager of the grain │
│ no class stand)                  depot now corrupted???) │
│                                                      │
│                                                      │
│ Qin Shutian                          the tax officer │
│ (reactionary Rightist)          (alien-class element) │
```

After holding this up to admire it, Yang Min'gao crumpled it up and chucked it into the waste-paper basket. But presently he retrieved it, smoothed it out, lit a match and burnt it.

In the lamplight he looked overworked, exhausted. After he had written his comments on this material from the Security Bureau, he could limber up on the verandah, have a wash, then sleep for a few hours. Finally he took another sheet of official stationery and picked up his pen, that pen which determined the fate of so many people. He wrote:

> Hibiscus lies on the border of three provinces. Being remote and complex, it has always been a political backwater. Whether or not such a "clique" exists requires careful investigation! Any new developments must be reported directly to the County Party Committee.

# Part 2
# The People of Hibiscus
## (1964)

## The Fourth Big Building

IN no time it was the spring of '64. A cold, wet, windy spring, bad for the crops. The sole surviving old hibiscus tree on the river bank flowered out of season, while the soap-bean in the street, which should have been a mass of flowers, failed to blossom. That gave rise to a lot of talk: Was it a good omen or a bad one? According to the old folk, when hibiscus blossomed in spring something out of the way would happen. They had seen it three times: first in 1909, when a plague killed off most of the townsfolk: secondly in 1933, when Hibiscus was flooded for a whole two weeks; thirdly in 1949, when the PLA came south to mop up bandits, and at last the poor stood up.... So really there was no knowing what fate had in store.

The whole town was on tenterhooks. But as now, fourteen years after Liberation, no fortune-tellers came to the market, some people consulted Qin Shutian of the Five Categories. Qin, who always seemed most enlightened and progressive, told them not to be so superstitious, linking social changes with natural calamities. And finally he quoted one of the revolutionary teachers' sayings that no illiterate country could build communism. Some felt he was showing off his erudition to stress the commune members' low level of consciousness.

But it does happen sometimes that changes in Nature coincide with important social events. Towards the end of February, the county committee sent a work team to Hibiscus led by the former manageress of the state eating-house. Li Guoxiang, simply dressed this time, her expression grave, for the first few days kept a low profile and stayed in Wang Qiushe's stilt-house, as he was a "poor peasant". This was what the Land Reform work teams had called "striking roots to establish contacts". The townsfolk always showed great respect to work teams sent from the county, but they were woefully ignorant about political changes, their wits dulled by their old way of life. Even Gu Yanshan and Li Mangeng, who had seen something of the world, expected to jog along in the old rut. Although dismayed by Li Guoxiang's reappearance, they did not take it too seriously. After all, they were the ones running Hibiscus. Besides, both of them were busy, Gu distributing good seeds of early rice, and Mangeng arranging ploughing.

So when the work team first moved into the stilt-house, this caused little stir in town. Everyone was more interested in the new house being built by Yuyin and her husband. Both of them had lost weight that winter, so busy were they getting a blueprint drawn, preparing building materials and hiring carpenters and masons. But losing weight only added to Sister Hibiscus's beauty. Her old inn was so rickety now that once the new house was built they meant to pull it down. The new house was just beside it, on the site they had bought for two hundred yuan from Wang Qiushe of the stilt-house. Having spent that money already, he regretted having sold his property so cheaply — he should have asked at least another hundred. Why, that was enough for a thousand bowls of beancurd! Now, whether he liked it or not, Li Guigui and Yuyin were building their new brick, tiled house with whitewashed walls. It had an impressive archway overlooking the flagstone street, and two French windows upstairs which opened on to a pretty balcony. Downstairs, stone steps led up to its red-lacquered gate. So this building combining Chinese and western features towered over its ramshackle neighbours, outshining even the department store, the grocery and the eating-house. It was the fourth big building in Hibiscus — and private property! Even before the scaffolding was dismantled, the townsfolk gathered there every day to admire it. Comrade Li Guoxiang, head of the work team, had mingled with the crowd on several occasions to jot down in her notebook the "masses' reactions".

"Fancy making enough from beancurd to build a mansion like this!"

"It's grander than the Salt Guild before Liberation."

"It's profiteers who get rich. This must have cost two or three thousand."

"What luck for a butcher like Li Guigui, moving in to live with his wife's family. . . . He must have done good in some earlier life!"

"Hu Yuyin's the smartest woman in town. Never put money in the bank but hoarded it on the sly. . . ."

When the new house was built, the old inn not yet pulled down, the hibiscus flowered out of season. To ward off bad luck, Yuyin decided to give a big feast for the cadres as well as the builders. She consulted her Brother Mangeng, the Party secretary, about this, and he gave his tacit consent. Then she invited Old Gu, the tax officer, the managers and accountants of the co-ops, department store, grocery and eating-house, besides some friends. Most people accepted gladly. She also made a point of inviting Li Guoxiang who disapproved of her, and the two other members of the work team. Li Guoxiang told her politely that the work team's rule was not to attend any feasts, but she promised to drop in later to see the new house. At least Yuyin was grateful for this show of courtesy.

On the first of March, at the crack of dawn firecrackers exploded in front of the new house, waking up the whole of Hibiscus. The big red-lacquered gate stood open, and on it was pasted a couplet in gold characters on red paper:

A hard-working couple have made a socialist fortune;

Our townsfolk add lustre to the people's commune.

An inscription on the lintel read: Live in peace and work hard. Needless to say, the calligraphy was Qin Shutian's.

All that morning people flocked in to offer congratulations, bringing mirrors and other gifts. Fire-crackers were let off continuously, till the flagstone street in front was covered with red and green paper like flowers scattered by a fairy. The air reeked of the heady smell of gunpowder, liquor and meat. At noon all the guests had arrived, and ten tables were laid in the new house and the old inn — what a scene of excitement! Old Gu, Secretary Mangeng, the tax officer, the managers of the co-ops and other cadres sat in the seats of honour.

Before the feast started Yuyin, both radiant and exhausted, begged Mangeng, "I can't drink and Guigui's shy in public, so will you act as host? You can hold your liquor. Get Manager Gu and the others to drink all they can. This is a red-letter day...."

"Don't worry. I'll start by making our 'soldier from the north' tipsy!"

"Crazy Qin has been a big help," Yuyin added. "I must show my appreciation to him differently."

"That's right, he's in a different category."

"Another thing, Brother Mangeng. Once we've moved into our new house and pulled down the old one, Guigui and I want to adopt a baby boy, if that's all right with the brigade...."

"My word, sister, drunk with joy, eh? What else do you want? Well, they're waiting for me to start...."

It was true, without drinking a drop, simply listening to the neighbours' congratulations and watching their smiling faces, Yuyin was drunk with joy.

The "soldier from the north" was in such high spirits that after one drink, prompted by Party Secretary Mangeng, he stood up, cup in hand, to speak. As always on formal occasions, he spoke with his old northern accent as if to stress the importance of what he said.

"Comrades! Today we're all as pleased as our hosts, coming here to celebrate the completion of their new house. An ordinary working couple, relying on their own hands, they saved enough money to build it. What does that mean? Hard work can lead to riches, a better life. We want to live well, not badly. That shows the superiority of our socialist system, the brilliance of our Party's leadership. So that's the first thing to remember as we tuck in. Secondly, as fellow townsfolk, what attitude should we take to the owners of this new house? Envy them? Try to imitate them? Or make snide remarks on the sly? I think we should imitate them and learn from them. Of course not everyone can keep a beancurd stall. But there are plenty of other ways to develop collective production and family side-lines. Thirdly, don't we talk a lot about building socialism and advancing to communism? Communism isn't something we can sit and wait for. A few years ago, we tried eating in the communal canteen, but it didn't work out. I think we'll know that communism is coming to Hibiscus when, apart from good food and clothes, every family builds a new house like this, even bigger and better than this! Instead of thatched roofs and adobe, instead of rickety wooden stilt-houses, we must have rows of neat storeyed buildings, a street as smart as in a city...."

As this was not a meeting, instead of applauding this speech the feasters laughed and cheered as they clinked cups. Of course a few were thinking: This is drunken talk. New houses and a good life — is that communism? According to the higher-ups, class struggle was the way to communism.

Next the tax officer proposed a toast. When he wished the owners of this new house a baby son and great prosperity, the guests all drank their health.

They were drinking home-brewed liquor distilled from grain which went down easily but then had a kick. And there were ten large dishes: chicken, duck, fish and meat. Old Gu and Mangeng let themselves go and had a good drinking-bout.

Certain canny people took a more detached view and noticed that Wang Qiushe, for the first time in his life, had not come to help out or join in the fun. That wasn't in character. Did he regret having sold his property so cheaply, so that he didn't want to see the new house built on it? Or was he too busy now with the work team in his stilt-house, having become an "activist" again? Another disquieting possibility was that he had some inside information and, knowing what was brewing, was on his guard.

## The Stilt-House

The stilt-house, once the property of a despot landlord, was elaborately built, entirely of wood. Overlooking the street, its front yard was now overgrown with brambles, while the plantains in its back yard were withering and the pomelo trees there were infested with insects. Its lower storey, with a sunken fire-place, had been the servants' quarters. The landlord had disported himself upstairs either in the front sitting-room or one of the three back bedrooms. Wang Qiushe lived downstairs, generally leaving the upper storey empty for any work teams which came to Hibiscus. Before he sold the grand carved bed upstairs, he had slept there for two or three years and dreamed many a pleasant dream of cuddling a singsong girl or drinking and feasting. Lying there, he used to wonder how many women the landlord had taken to that bed: young, middle-aged, plump, slim. Later on the fellow had died a painful death from syphilis. Serve him right! But Wang fancied the bed still smelt of cosmetics and scent.

Gradually Wang Qiushe developed bad habits. On clear moonlight nights he used to caper about the sitting-room as the landlord was said to have done, or sprawl on the bed hugging a pillow as if it were his sweetheart. "Sing your sugar daddy a song, love!" The gentry in the old days had thought it smart to sing arias from Beijing opera; but as Wang could not, he sang snatches of local operas. Sometimes he padded barefoot through the sitting-room and bedrooms as if chasing after a woman. He skirted the pillars, jumped over stools and crawled under the table, cursing, "Little slut! Little devil!" When worn out by this he flopped down on the grand carved bed like a dead snake, unable to move. Then, in frustration, he wept.

"That landlord had food, liquor, women ... but all I can do is dream...."

For a time, the neighbours hearing this commotion and his shrieks of laughter or curses, thought the place must be haunted by a fox-fairy, who had bewitched Wang Qiushe to punish him for his bad ways. At first some of them had proposed matches to him, but now they no longer did. And most young women and girls would lower their heads and hurry past the stilt-house, to avoid coming under the influence of its "black magic". Later Wang claimed to have met bewitching fox-fairies lovelier than all the girls in town — except for Hu Yiyin the beancurd pedlar. However, he stopped sleeping upstairs, not from fear of fairies but for fear of going crazy. And soon it was said in town that the owner of the stilt-house had not seen any fairies but was infatuated with Sister Hibiscus and had hung around the old inn till Li Guigui with his chopper drove him away. But as Yuyin and her husband were highly thought of, such rumours were not believed.

As Wang neglected the upkeep of the stilt-house,

when Li Guoxiang and her two colleagues moved in it was tilting precariously, propped up with three wooden buttresses. To each of these was fastened a heavy stone, which on dark nights looked like three corpses hanging there — a sight to make your flesh creep. The floors crawling with insects were black, with weeds growing through their cracks like a green inlaid design. And behind the house matted creepers reached up the windows.

Li Guoxiang was touched by this rickety house and yard overgrown with weeds, shocked to find Wang Qiushe, the "Land Reform activist", still so badly off fifteen years after Liberation. What was the problem? During the three hard years, capitalism had reared its ugly head. Unless they launched a new movement and grasped class struggle, there was bound to be a new polarization in the countryside with the rich becoming richer, the poor poorer. The Party would turn revisionist, the fruits of the revolution would be lost, there would be a restoration of capitalism with the landlords and bourgeoisie seizing power again, and true Communists would have to take to the mountains to fight guerrilla warfare.... The sight of Wang Qiushe's broken pan and cracked bowl brought the tears to her eyes, so deep was her class feeling! She and her colleagues spent two yuan apiece to buy him a bright aluminium pan, plastic chopsticks and ten rice bowls. They also set to work to clean up the back yard and save the half-dead plantains and pomelo trees. In doing this Li Guoxiang raised blood-blisters on her hands and scratched both her wrists. When the stilt-house had been cleaned up, she pasted a red couplet on its gate:

Never forget class struggle,
Never stop criticizing capitalism.

In order to "strike root" in the town the work team
was in no hurry to call meetings, put up slogans or mo-
bilize the masses. First they investigated the political
status of all the cadres and townsfolk, to see with whom
they should unite, which people needed to be re-educated, and which should be isolated and attacked.
One day Li Guoxiang sent her colleagues to visit
"poor peasants" in town while she stayed in the stilt-
house to read Wang Qiushe some directives. In her
previous dealings with him she had been favourably
impressed by his poverty, his hatred of the oppressors,
his firm class stand and his obedience to the higher-ups.
He was not bad-looking either, strong, cheerful and
pleasant. Better still, he was quick on the uptake, had
a ready tongue and a certain organizing ability. It is
wrong to judge a man by appearances. Wang was
shabbily dressed now; but if he wore a cadre's uniform,
a shirt with a white collar and brown army gum-shoes,
he would look no worse than a section chief in the county. She decided to use him as a model in the coming
movement; so that she herself would be known throughout the county for her skilled handling of this campaign
in Hibiscus.

As Li Guoxiang read out the document and made
these plans, she eyed Wang Qiushe appraisingly from
time to time. He, of course, had no idea of her
intentions. When she read the directives on "purifying"
the class ranks, checking up on everybody's status, and
cleaning up the economy, his eyes lit up. He could not
resist asking her:

"Team Leader Li, is this to be a second Land Reform?"

"A second Land Reform? Yes, we'll be relying on poor peasants and hired hands to crush the landlords, rich peasants, counter-revolutionaries, bad elements and Rightists, as well as the new bourgeois elements!"

"Will people be reclassified, Team Leader Li?"

"It's a tricky situation. Where Land Reform wasn't carried out thoroughly, our class ranks will have to be overhauled. I like the way you use your brain, Old Wang."

"There's one thing I don't understand. Does cleaning up the economy apply to the property of each family?"

He stared unblinkingly at Li Guoxiang, tempted to ask if there would be another sharing out of property. Rather embarrassed by his scrutiny, she looked away as she went on explaining:

"We'll go through the brigade's accounts for these last few years, check up on any corruption among cadres, check up on the traders who have given up farming, and the property of speculators. We'll put on a class exhibition, and settle accounts politically as well as in the economic field."

"Fine! I'm all for such a movement. You can count on me."

Wang sprang excitedly to his feet. This seemed too good to be true — a second Land Reform. Those dolts who had got good land, buffaloes and tools last time had worked hard and saved money to build a house or get rich. He, Wang Qiushe had seen further. Still a poor peasant, he could struggle against them. In jubilation he caught hold of the team leader's hands.

"Team Leader Li, I'm at your service. I'll do whatever the work team says."

Li Guoxiang pulled her hands away. Disgusting!

"Sit down!" she said sternly. "Don't forget yourself or the impression you're making."

Wang flushed and sat down.

"Beg pardon! I was so carried away by that directive I forgot you were a woman, Team Leader Li. . . ."

"Don't talk nonsense. Let's get back to business." She smiled tolerantly, smoothing back her hair. "You know this town. Who are the newly rich here?"

"You mean among cadres? Or ordinary households? . . . One of the cadres protects capitalist elements. He sells Hu Yuyin sixty pounds of rice seconds to make beancurd for each market, and out of their profits they've built a big house. But he has a good record and he's highly respected. You may have trouble if you tackle him."

"If he's really done wrong, we're not afraid to touch the tiger's backside. Who else is there?"

"The tax officer. They say he comes from a bureaucrat landlord family and hates the poor and lower-middle peasants. He often calls me a bum, one of the lumpen proletariat. . . ."

"Ha, slandering poor peasants is slandering the revolution. Who else?"

"Then there's Li Mangeng, secretary of the brigade. He has a wobbly stand, gets the bad element Qin Shutian to write slogans and round up the Five Categories. And he calls Hu Yuyin who sells beancurd his sister. He's in cahoots with the managers of the grain depot and supply and marketing co-op. They're the ones who run Hibiscus. . . ."

Wang Qiushe had told the truth. These local heads did call him a greedy loafer who was afraid of hard work. Li Mangeng had gone even further, refusing him relief grain and relief clothing — the fellow had no class feeling! As long as they were in charge he could never really stand up. Thank Heaven the government had sent this work team to speak up for the poor and topple the rich and powerful!

Li Guoxiang made notes of all he had to tell her about the local cadres. And Wang Qiushe was a mine of information. He had a good memory, knew which townsfolk were related or connected, which had quarrelled, which had plundered another family's hen-coop or been cursed by someone else's wife, which had a child who didn't take after his father.... He reeled all this off in circumstantial detail, citing places, witnesses, dates. The team leader began to be quite impressed by this "activist" who knew all about Hibiscus.

"These last few years, because of the state's temporary difficulties, commercial rules have been relaxed and the markets have got out of hand," she said. "Which family has made the most money by trading here?"

"Need you ask? Hu Yuyin, who's built that big new house. She set up a beancurd stall, counting on her good looks to attract customers. Made a pile. She's really smart. On good terms with most everyone in town. And the cadres...."

"What's their attitude to her?" The team leader felt very curious about this.

"They like her pretty face! Secretary Li treats her so well, his wife is jealous. The manager of the grain

depot supplies her with rice seconds, the tax-officer is
like a brother to her, just taxing her one yuan each
market-day. Even that bad element Qin Shutian is
thick with her, and learned all sorts of old folk-songs
from her to make out that socialism is feudalistic. I ask
you, how low can you sink."

From this conversation Li Guoxiang gained invalu-
able first-hand material. She decided that the owner of
the stilt-house had great potential and she must try to
groom him in this movement.

Two weeks later the work team had the low-down on
every family in Hibiscus. However, they had not yet
mobilized the masses. They decided to set about this
by contrasting the bitter past with the sweet present,
to arouse the townsfolks' class feeling. First they would
share a meal recalling their former wretchedness, then
sing songs about it, and put on an exhibition of class
struggle in the brigade. This exhibition would have two
parts: pre-Liberation and post-Liberation. For the first
part they needed certain exhibits: a tattered quilt, a
ragged padded jacket, an old basket, a stick with which
to beat dogs, a chipped bowl.

But where could they find such things fifteen years
after Liberation now that everybody was so much better off? At the time of Land Reform the poor had been
so happy to have stood up, all they wanted to do was
to farm the good land they had received and race ahead
down the road to socialism; so they had thrown all that
junk away, sick of the sight of it, not foreseeing that
it would be wanted so much later for an exhibition
contrasting past and present. They should have looked
further ahead. The worse off places were, the more

they should recall the wretched past to remind themselves how much better off they were now. Of course there were minor faults in today's collective economy, but that was no reason for them to complain or lose heart. It was no good either comparing themselves with communes doing better.

Li Guoxiang intended to put on this exhibition to get the movement going. But she could find no pre-Liberation exhibits until suddenly she had the bright idea of consulting the activist. Wang Qiushe hesitated a moment, then said:

"Well, there are some things you might use. . . ."

"Hurry up and fetch them."

Li Guoxiang smiled, a weight lifted from her mind, as her trusty henchman rummaged in one corner.

Presently, covered with dust, he brought a crate of things for her to inspect: a ragged old quilt, a filthy, threadbare padded jacket, a broken basket and a badly chipped bowl. All that was missing was a stick, but that could be found anywhere.

"Aha, that's solved my problem. Trust you, Old Wang!" she approved cheerfully.

"But the quilt and jacket were government relief I got after Liberation. . . ." he confessed.

"Are you joking? This is a serious political task," she answered sharply. "I've been to big museums in Hengzhou and Guangzhou where most exhibits in the cabinets are models or replicas."

## A Woman's Reckoning

Word went round that the work team was going to take over Sister Hibiscus's beancurd stall and her husband's cleaver. Where this talk started there is no knowing. But people love to gossip just as bees and butterflies spread pollen in spring — this is second nature to them. And they often embroider this gossip so that it grows increasingly fantastic, until they are distracted by some new rumour.

Their neighbours' significant glances and whispered comments preyed upon the minds of Hu Yuyin and her husband, making her feel desperate, making him scared stiff. Guigui lost his appetite. No wonder politicians use public opinion as a weapon and conduct a publicity campaign before taking any action.

"Good heavens!" Yuyin complained. "Other husbands are pillars of strength. But if *we* have any trouble you're more timid than a woman, too scared to eat!"

"Yuyin, I, we didn't think...." Guigui faltered. "In the new society, people shouldn't build themselves houses. Some families tightened their belts a few years before Land Reform, skimping and saving to buy themselves fields and orchards; but then they were labelled as landlords and rich peasants, weren't they?"

"What do you think we should do?" Yuyin clenched her teeth.

"Let's not wait for the work team to pounce on us, but hurry up and get this new house off our hands ... even selling it at a loss. We're fated to live in this dump." Guigui's eyes were flickering this way and that.

"You big shit!" Yuyin stabbed at him furiously with her chopsticks, leaving two red marks on his forehead. "Landlords and rich peasants collected rent! They loaned money at high interest, exploited their hired hands! Does a butcher exploit anyone? Do I exploit anyone by selling beancurd? Sell our new house? Fated to live in a dump, are we? How can you even think of such a thing! Here we've worked our fingers to the bone, nearly wearing out the mill handle and the cauldron, and you say: Sell the new house! Heavens, other men fight in wars to win a country, mine can't even hold on to a house...."

Guigui felt his forehead — beads of blood were oozing from where she had stabbed it. Yuyin's eyes filled with tears of remorse. In the eight years of their marriage never before had they quarrelled. Having no child, she had mothered her husband instead; indeed, his very weakness had made her more protective, more solicitous for him. To her, Guigui was her husband, her brother, sometimes even her son — and now she had bloodied his forehead! She hastily put down her bowl and went over to clasp his head in her arms.

"You fool, you! Can't you even say if it hurts?"

Guigui, far from losing his temper, rested his head on her breast. "It doesn't really hurt, Yuyin. I just suggested selling the new house, but it's up to you to decide. What you say goes.... You're my family, my home.... With you, I'm not afraid of anything... not afraid to go begging, I swear it...."

Yuyin held him close, as if to shield him from danger, and she shed tears. Yes, as a countrywoman, a stall-holder, her world was very restricted. She and her husband were everything to each other. It was for each other that they had worked so hard, putting up with so many hardships.

"Yuyin, you mustn't think me such a rat. I do have guts. If you told me to kill someone for our new house, I'd do it with my cleaver. I know I could...." His eyes closed, Guigui was muttering as if in his sleep — and in such a lawless way!

Yuyin hastily stopped his mouth. "Are you crazy, talking like that? It's a crime even to think of such a thing." Turning away from him she wiped her eyes.

"I just said that to show you, Yuyin.... I'm not going to kill anybody...."

"Either you want to sell our new house, or you want to risk your neck. A little bit of gossip and you're scared stiff.... If real trouble happened, how could you cope?"

"The worst they can do is kill us."

This angered Yuyin again. She raised her hand to slap him, then lowered it. She felt crushed, the situation was so serious. But for all her gentle ways she had determination. She reached a decision:

"I'll go and see Li Guoxiang, the head of the work team, to ask if they really mean to take over my bean-curd stall and your cleaver.... I think the work team members sent from above are mostly like Manager Gu, on the side of us underdogs."

Guigui watched her admiringly. In any pinch, his wife was always the one who knew what to do. Their roles as husband and wife had been reversed.

As she combed her hair Yuyin wondered how to broach the matter to the team leader without annoying her or giving anyone a handle against her. But just before setting out she heard a pleasant woman's voice outside:

"Is Hu Yuyin at home? There's no market today."

Yuyin went to the gate and discovered Li Guoxiang there, smiling. What a coincidence! She hastily ushered her in. Li Guoxiang appeared more affluent, less wrinkled, than she had as manageress of the eating-house. Her present job called for brains, not physical exertion, and as she lived quite comfortably at thirty-three she still looked fairly young.

Guigui was relieved to see that she had come alone and seemed friendly. He made haste to brew tea and offer her peanuts and melon seeds. This done he threw his wife a glance and said with a sheepish smile, "Make yourself at home, Team Leader Li." Then he took his hoe from behind the door and went off to his vegetable plot.

Li Guoxiang sipped her tea and asked half jokingly, "Is your husband so shy of strangers that he has to run off like a savage?"

"Oh, him, he's dumb." Flushing, Yuyin offered her peanuts and melon seeds, thinking: What do you, an old spinster, know about men that you call them savages?

"I've come today from the work team to see over your new house. And to discuss a couple of things with you. Don't worry, we're old acquaintances, but we can't allow personal considerations to interfere with public business." Taking a handful of melon seeds she stood up.

Yuyin had turned pale. She felt rather tense. This visit was certainly ominous. The team leader could not have come to see their new house out of curiosity. But Yuyin kept a grip on herself as with a forced smile she led Li Guoxiang out and opened the red-lacquered gate of the new house. The inside smelt of new wood and of varnish. As the team leader inspected the hall, the wing-rooms, kitchen, store-room, and the pigsty, hen-coop and lavatory in the back yard, she kept commenting, "Not bad, not bad." Then they went upstairs to see the bright, spacious bedroom with its big wardrobe, four-poster bed, chest of drawers, desk, round table and armchairs. This shiny new furniture stood out in pleasant contrast to the gleaming whitewashed walls.

"Not bad, not bad," Li Guoxiang approved, nodding her head as if most impressed.

Yuyin watched her reactions carefully, but could not make out what she was really thinking. Finally she opened the French windows and they went out to the balcony which overlooked the town. Leaning on the balustrade Li Guoxiang had the air of a high official on a reviewing stand. From here she could see the old houses of adobe and brick as well as the ramshackle stilt-house, so different from this fine new building, showing the gulf between wealth and poverty.

Back in the bedroom, Li Guoxiang sat down in front of the desk by the window. Yuyin, standing beside her, saw that Team Leader Li had taken out a notebook and fountain-pen.

"Sit down, sit down. Just the two of us, let's have a talk." Li Guoxiang was acting as if the house were hers.

Yuyin drew up a square stool. Confronted by this team leader with her notebook, she felt in an inferior position; so it was appropriate for her to sit on a stool while the other sat in an armchair.

"Hu Yuyin, as you must know, our work team from the county has come here to launch a Four Clean-ups Movement," began Li Guoxiang formally. "First we have to assess each family's political and financial situation. You're neither the first family we're investigating, nor the last. If you come clean to the work team, it shows your trust in the Party. Understand?"

Yuyin nodded, though completely at sea.

"I've drawn up a preliminary reckoning for you and have come here to check it out. You can point out any discrepancies there are." Li Guoxiang looked hard at Yuyin.

Yuyin nodded, thinking that this saved her trouble. If called on for a reckoning she might have panicked. And the team leader's attitude was fairly friendly, she wasn't glaring at her as if haranguing the Five Categories.

"In the second half of 1961, Hibiscus market changed from once a fortnight to once every five days. That's six markets a month, right?" Li Guoxiang eyed Yuyin.

Again Yuyin nodded in silence. She had no idea why the team leader was harking so far back.

"That makes two years and nine months up to February this year," Li Guoxiang went on, consulting her notebook. "In other words, thirty-three months in all. A hundred and ninety-eight markets, right?"

Too stupefied to nod, Yuyin sensed that this was an interrogation.

"You use about fifty pounds of rice to make beancurd for each market. Some people call this a family sideline, but we won't go into that now. You must sell about ten bowls of beancurd for each pound of rice. If you sell five hundred bowls at each market, you should make approximately fifty yuan. Six markets a month, you make three hundred yuan. From that we can deduct a hundred, say, for your expenses. So you still make two hundred yuan a month! That, incidentally, is as much as the salary of a provincial secretary. So your annual income is 2,400 yuan. In two years and nine months you must have made 6,600 yuan!"

Yuyin was amazed by this detailed reckoning. Heavens, she had never worked it out herself. . . . She felt as if struck by lightning.

"Trading in a small way, I never figured that out. . . . We just muddled along, and what money we put by we spent on this house. . . . I've got a trading licence, Team Leader Li. I got permission from the authorities. . . ."

"We're not saying you broke the law or exploited anyone." Li Guoxiang's expression was cryptic. "Doesn't it say on that red couplet on your gate, 'Make a socialist fortune'? I'm told that was written by the Five-Categories element Qin Shutian. Don't be upset, I'm just getting to the bottom of this."

Yuyin, first alarmed, now looked numbed and apathetic. Her lips clamped together, she stared at the floor. The team leader went on calmly:

"Another thing. The manager of the grain depot, Gu Yanshan, supplied you with sixty pounds of good rice for each market, didn't he?" She was looking sterner now, as if interrogating a loose woman.

"Not *good* rice!" exclaimed Yuyin. "Seconds, sweepings from the grain depot. I always have to sieve it to get rid of the sand, husks and dirt. And I'm not the only one Manager Gu supplies. Lots of organizations and private families buy seconds to feed their pigs. . . . I bought it first for our pigs, then used it later for this little side-line. . . ." At mention of Manager Gu, Yuyin had roused herself from her apathy. Old Gu was a good man. If she had done something wrong, she mustn't involve him.

"That's why I just reckoned you use fifty pounds of rice to make beancurd. I deducted ten pounds for husks, grit and sand. I'm making allowances for you. And those people who buy rice seconds to fatten their pigs sell them to the state, whereas you change yours into a commodity which you sell for a profit."

This silenced Yuyin. And the team leader went on calmly, referring to her notebook:

"Six markets a month, sixty pounds each market-day, a hundred and ninety-eight markets in two years and nine months. Manager Gu has supplied you altogether with 11,880 pounds of rice. A staggering amount! Still, that's another question. Although you're involved, the main responsibility isn't yours."

After this reckoning Li Guoxiang wrote in her notebook, "This has been confirmed by Hu Yuyin, the beancurd pedlar." She then left. Yuyin saw her off, too frantic even to offer her any refreshments.

That evening Yuyin told her husband the team leader's estimate that they had bought over ten thousand pounds of rice and made 6,600 yuan. They were as nervous as two profiteers on the eve of a second Land Reform. But the profiteers in the old society were now in the Five Categories, they stank, and no one was afraid of them. Yuyin and her husband had made a bit of money in the new society. Did that mean they would be reclassified as new landlords or rich peasants?

After this, Yuyin and Guigui found it hard to sleep at night. They accepted that they were destined to live in a dump. Though thieves might break in here, they felt it was politically more secure. They stopped longing for a child, secretly glad that they had none. Otherwise their child would have been treated as a little Five-Categories element, poor thing!

# Killing the Chicken to Frighten the Monkey

That evening, the work team called its first mass meeting in front of the stage in the market-place. The guttering paraffin lamp had been repaired and cast a bright light, making people's faces seem livid. In the past the leading figures in the town would have been up on the stage; but now the manager of the grain depot, the Party secretary and tax officer were sitting below on stools they had brought or on bricks. Yuyin and Guigui sat immediately behind them, as if hoping for their protection. The only people on the stage were the work team. The townsfolk, intrigued and puzzled by this new departure, wanted to squeeze forward for a closer look. Some made a detour to the front of the stage to locate the "soldier from the north" and Secretary Mangeng.

Another new departure was that Li Guoxiang, presiding at the meeting, did not make the usual opening speech about the excellent international and domestic situation before getting down to business. First one of the work team read out three circulars. That from the province announced that a bad character hostile to the Party had viciously attacked the Four Clean-ups Movement and incited some backward people to beat up the work team. For this serious crime he had been sentenced to fifteen years of hard labour. The circular from the district announced that a member of the Party committee of a certain commune and the Party secretary of one brigade had for years been using his power to protect the Five Categories. When a work team was sent there he had stormed and raged, refusing to answer questions; so he had been dismissed from his post, expelled from the Party and made to work under mass supervision. The circular from the county announced that a pedlar in one commune, who had been a prostitute before Liberation and had long been profiteering, had bribed the cadres to help her scrape through this movement. She had been paraded and struggled against to educate the cadres and Party members.

The effect of these announcements was uncanny: at once absolute silence reigned, as if a sudden blizzard had frozen everyone attending the meeting. Gu Yanshan, Li Mangeng and the others who normally ran Hibiscus could only stare, dumbfounded.

"Fetch the bourgeois Rightist Qin Shutian!" one of the work team thundered.

At once Wang Qiushe and a militiaman marched Qin Shutian to the stage. There was a stir of excitement, but soon it subsided. Qin Shutian, his hands at his sides and his head lowered, was too dazzled by the bright light to open his eyes.

Li Guoxiang had been sitting by the square table on the stage. Now she walked forward, smoothing back her hair, and pointed at Qin Shutian. With a clear local accent she said:

"This is the notorious Qin Shutian, Crazy Qin of Hibiscus. The poor and lower-middle peasants here, the revolutionary masses, hate landlords and rich peasants. But do you hate this class enemy? I call on all cadres, Communists and Youth League members to say what you think of him. During the three hard years, this Qin Shutian cut quite a dash, writing couplets and slogans, playing instruments and singing. At every marriage and feast, he was always invited to play in the band. When you put on a dragon dance, he always took part. When you met him on the road, how many of you greeted him or gave him a cigarette? How many of you listened to those decadent stories he told in the fields, using the past to satirize the present? Your children, too young to have been oppressed or exploited, how many of them called him 'Uncle Qin'?"

Li Guoxiang had not raised her voice, speaking calmly and reasonably. The atmosphere seemed icy, with all present holding their breath. Gu Yanshan, Mangeng, Yuyin and her husband felt that a gulf was yawning at their feet.

"Many extraordinary things have happened, comrades!" Li Guoxiang went on slowly, as if chatting to them. She had obviously mastered the art of struggle and prided herself on her ability to sway the masses. "Not long ago, a pedlar in our Hibiscus built a brand-new storeyed house. Some of you have pointed out that it's grander than the two biggest shops here before Liberation. We should ask: Just how much money has that pedlar made these last few years? Whose money was it? And where did she get the rice to make her beancurd? But we won't go into that now. Who wrote the couplet on her red-lacquered gate? Qin Shutian, recite that couplet."

Qin raised his head to glance at her from the corner of his eyes. "I wrote it," he answered. "It says, 'A hard-working couple have made a socialist fortune. Our townsfolk add lustre to the people's commune.' On the lintel. . . ."

"That's a reactionary couplet, comrades!" She signed to Qin to keep quiet, then raised her voice. " 'A hard-working couple have made a socialist fortune.' Doesn't that stink? How can individuals building socialism make a fortune? In the past we talked about 'ill-gotten gains' but he's made up this reactionary slogan 'a socialist fortune' to fool you. This is an attack on the people's commune's collective economy! In our Hibiscus today, the rich build big houses, the poor sell their land — what does this mean? Just think it over, comrades. And that second line 'Our townsfolk add lustre to the people's commune' is even more blatant. Who are these townsfolk? Are they genuine poor and lower-middle peasants, or are they people with a dirty past and disreputable connections? We have learned that they made up a jingle to slander our policy and our class line:

The government has its quirks;
It trusts a slacker who shirks,
Ignores those who really work,
And those who do well it pulls up with a jerk.

Is this just backward talk? How can people like this add lustre to the people's commune? The people's commune is paradise, it's splendid. It doesn't need private ownership to add lustre to it. These people want to bring down our regime. They're against the Party and socialism, comrades. And a reactionary couplet like this is openly pasted up in our town! Is the owner of that new house here or not? Don't tear that couplet down. We'll keep it as negative material for all of you to read three times a day. Don't underestimate the written word, comrades. It's often used by class enemies as a weapon."

Unconvinced by this, Qin Shutian looked up at her. At once Wang Qiushe behind him rammed his head down. And some activists shouted, "Make Qin Shutian kneel down!"

"Can we let him keep standing there?" another protested.

There was a pause before a voice seconded, "No, we can't!"

Trembling, Crazy Qin looked pleadingly at the Party secretary, but Mangeng had lowered his head and paid no attention. Behind him Sister Hibiscus and her husband were staring frantically round. Qin's legs buckled and he knelt down.

"You can stand up, Qin Shutian," said Li Guoxiang to everyone's surprise. But of course, as a cadre sent from above she adhered to the policy for struggle meetings.

Qin stood up as before, hands at his sides, head lowered. Only his trouser knees were now covered with dust.

"Now we'll go on criticizing you, Qin Shutian, to tear off your mask and expose you to the masses," she continued. "The older generation all know the story of the hero and thieving scholar Xiao Rang in the novel *Outlaws of the Marsh*. Some of our cadres have treated Qin Shutian as a good scholar. Aren't the walls and rocks here covered with the slogans he has written? With over a hundred households in Hibiscus, is everyone illiterate except for this Five-Categories element? Why add to his prestige? Tell us, Qin Shutian, who honoured you like this?"

Crazy Qin stole a glance at Secretary Mangeng. "It was the brigade ... brigade...."

"All right, that's enough." Li Guoxiang knew the time was ripe to raise a more serious problem. "Qin

Shutian! Tell the revolutionary masses your class status."

"A bad element, bad element," he said.

"A bad element indeed! Comrades, the work team has uncovered a plot. Found out in the course of our investigations that Qin Shutian is not a bad element but a vicious Rightist, who wrote a reactionary song-and-dance drama to attack the Party and socialism. Who did him the good turn of changing him from a Rightist into a bad element who ran after women? A list of the Five Categories is kept in the County Public Security Bureau. This is a serious breach of law and discipline!"

Here Li Guoxiang paused. Like all experienced speakers she knew when to give her audience a moment to think, to realize the enormity of some problem, or to memorize some maxim.

The meeting-place buzzed with comments and exclamations.

"Commune members!" The team leader lowered her voice again. "Many, many strange things have happened in Hibiscus. Qin Shutian has a special status as the head of all the Five Categories here. He's been put over them. Just think, how could our cadres give an important task like that to a Rightist? It's the duty and right of the poor and lower-middle peasants to supervise and remould the Five Categories. But some of our cadres gave this right to a class enemy. What does this mean, comrades? It means drawing no distinction between the enemy and ourselves — a complete loss of class stand. Today our work team has singled out Qin Shutian as a target, a negative example, and a mirror to show our cadres and Party members which side they're on!"

She then led them in shouting slogans, had the Right-

ist Qin Shutian marched out and ordered the Five Categories and their families to leave.

By way of conclusion Team Leader Li said:

"Now that the class enemies have left, I have something to add." She smoothed her hair gracefully, her
voice much softer. "Commune members, a sharp class
struggle, a complex struggle to the death, is going to
unfold in Hibiscus. The work team will plunge into this
struggle whole-heartedly with you. During the hard
years when policies were relaxed, some Party members,
cadres and commune members made certain mistakes
— never mind. Our policy is: Own up, pay back what
you've embezzled, and make a fresh start. What if
some people refuse to admit their faults? They'll be
dealt with according to the law and Party discipline.
Otherwise, the landlords, rich peasants, counter-revolutionaries, bad elements and Rightists will get out of
hand with Party members in cahoots with them; and if
our cadres and the masses do nothing about this, before
long our Party will turn revisionist, and the landlords
and bourgeoisie will seize power again!"

Yuyin and Guigui went back to the inn completely
panic-stricken. They realized that their new house was
doomed. Before they had spent a single night there it
had been the ruin of them. Even if they were willing
to stay on in this dump, they no longer had any sense
of security. For what upset them most was the real-
ization that Manager Gu and Secretary Mangeng were
going to be victimized too by the team leader. Like
clay idols fording a river, they would hardly be able
to save themselves, let alone anyone else.

Trembling with fright Guigui stared, wild-eyed, at his wife.

Yuyin sat on a bamboo chair reflecting that if the two of them panicked, their only way out was to hang themselves.

"I tell you what, there's no time to be lost. They may come any evening to raid us. I'll give that money we have left to Brother Mangeng to keep. Otherwise it will land us in trouble. . . ." She spoke in a low voice, her eyes on their door.

"Mangeng? Didn't you hear what he did for Crazy Qin? . . . The team leader was gunning for him most of the time, killing the chicken to frighten the monkey. . . ."

"Never mind. He's in the Party. At most he'll get a bashing and write a self-criticism. What can they do to an ex-PLA man?"

"We don't want to get other people into trouble."

"He's my adopted brother. The only person we can count on."

"All right. And let's stop selling beancurd before they take over the stall. You'd better go away till all this blows over. I've got some distant relatives in Xiuzhou in Guangxi. We've been out of touch for over ten years, so nobody here knows about them. . . ."

## Party Secretary Mangeng

Secretary Mangeng's home, these last few days, has been the scene of rows and recriminations. His strapping wife, known as Peppery, was an able-bodied field worker and a capable housekeeper. The previous year her husband had talked himself hoarse to publicize the advantages of late marriage and birth control, but his wife bred like a rabbit. Of her six children, four had survived, all girls. Some commune members teased her, "As the secretary's wife, you ought to take the lead in family planning!" Her arms akimbo she would retort, "Me take the lead? If I had my way, I'd produce a whole squad of militiawomen...."

The year that Li Mangeng married he had thought his wife rather crude with her big hands and feet. When she rolled up her sleeves and trouser-legs she showed all the strength of a man. She couldn't compare with lovely Hu Yuyin. The old folk said that beauties were always ill-fated. What would Yuyin's fate be? He had no way of knowing, not being a fortune teller. But after his wife had given birth to two daughters, he began to appreciate her good qualities. Field work, house-work, nursing babies — nothing tired her or stopped her singing. Up before it was light, at night she snored as soundly as a man or a hefty cow. Then she had four more babies, without even going to the commune hospital. He came to the conclusion, "Living with a woman like this you know where you are. She saves me a lot of worry." If she had a fault it was her fecundity.

Peppery seldom made a scene. But she wasn't too easy in her mind about him working outside. And she was afraid he might be led astray by Hu Yuyin whom he had taken as his "sister" before their marriage, because she was as lovely as a fairy. Watching carefully for two years she could see no sign that they were carrying on. However, she didn't relax her vigilance. Although she said nothing she made it clear that she had her eye on him — he had better watch out. Sometimes she said half jokingly, "Have you been up to some dirty business again with that sister of yours? You should have some self-respect."

"Are you asking for a beating?"

"I'm just reminding you that your roots are here. Her husband may be a sap but his cleaver is sharp!"

"Stop shitting through your yellow teeth!"

"You love that bitch's white teeth, don't you?"

Not until Mangeng raised his fist would she pipe down.

When they got back from the meeting that evening, Peppery scolded:

"Party secretary! Over half the work team leader said was aimed at you! Did you take that in?"

His face grim, Mangeng sat down on a bench to twist a tobacco spill.

"What are you really up to with that sister of yours who sells beancurd? Why did you lose your class stand with Crazy Qin? That team leader all but named you by name. What a rum creature she is, not like a girl or a married woman either." Peppery sat herself down on the other end of the bench.

"Stop farting, will you? Wasn't the stink at the meeting enough for you!" Mangeng scowled at his wife.

"Don't come the big boss over *me*! Why not put up a fight outside if you're such a fine fellow?" Peppery was not giving in.

"Will you lay off?" Mangeng rounded on her, his face furious. "Itching for a clout, are you?"

Peppery always had enough sense to back down when he seemed about to explode. So although in the last eight years they had often squabbled, as he knew that she wouldn't take anything lying down and she knew that he was the stronger, they had seldom come to blows. Now she sprang up from the bench, making it tilt and landing Mangeng on the floor.

"Serves you right!" crowed Peppery as she slipped into the bedroom.

He jumped up and chased her to the bedroom door. "You bitch! See if I don't clobber you!"

She pulled the door nearly shut. "Don't you dare! Who told you to sit on that side? You can't blame me for your fall."

Normally, whenever she teased him, he would calm down and lower his raised fist.

But this evening he could not calm down. His wife's remarks had reminded him of the team leader's challenge: Which side are you on? Had he really sided with the landlords, rich peasants, counter-revolutionaries, bad elements, Rightists and bourgeoisie? Or encouraged capitalism by supporting Sister Yuyin's beancurd stall? Now that she'd made enough money to build a new house, the best in the whole town, did that mean she'd exploited people to get rich quick? Did it make her a new rich peasant? As for changing Qin Shutian's status from that of Rightist to bad element, he had announced this at a mass meeting without taking the business seriously enough, he hadn't gone through any formal procedures. Was the team leader right in calling a bad element less vicious than a Rightist? To him, they were much of a muchness — both poisonous snakes. And had he really favoured a class enemy by giving Qin the job of writing slogans?

The next evening, Peppery had taken a bucket of swill to feed the pigs as Mangeng, just back from a struggle meeting in the commune, washed his feet in the doorway, when Yuyin came anxiously along and handed him a package wrapped in oilpaper. She told him it was 1,500 yuan, and asked him to keep it for her. If he was short of money he could spend some. Yuyin looked distraught, not her usual self at all, with tousled hair and wearing a black gown. Not even sitting down to rest, she dashed frantically off, afraid to let anyone see her.

As Mangeng knew this money could not be banked, he followed the local custom of hiding it in the crack of a big brick upstairs without even counting it. Regarding money matters, he and Yuyin trusted each other implicitly. And this method of keeping money was no secret in town — it was common. Thieves would have to dismantle the walls to find the hoard. It was insects and rats that had to be guarded against.

Mangeng had meant to keep this from his wife, but she saw the dust on his clothes when he came downstairs, and his refusal to answer any questions only increased her suspicions. She wept and sobbed, complaining that they had been married all these years, she had borne four daughters for him, yet he treated her like a thief.... Mangeng's heart was melted by her tears, and he felt he could confide in his own wife.

But there he was wrong. When he disclosed this secret to her in bed, Peppery sprang up abruptly.

"Fine! You'll be the ruin of us! You're asking for trouble, you wretch! I've been a good wife to you but you're bewitched by that tramp!" She shrieked at him as if possessed by a devil.

"What's there to scream about? Have some self-respect, woman!" Mangeng got up to bellow back at her.

"What's there to scream about! When you've made me a tortoise's wife! Tomorrow I'll go and have it out with that bitch!" Her hair down, wearing only thin underclothes, Peppery pounded her thighs as she wept and stormed at him.

"Will you shut up? You bitch! I consult you and you carry on as if the sky were falling, our family finished!" Mangeng's eyes were nearly popping out of his head, but he tried to control his anger for fear of rousing the neighbours and causing a scandal.

"Tell me straight, what's that bitch Hu Yuyin to you? Is she your wife or am I? I'm sick of the way you've ogled each other for years."

"I'll stop your stinking mouth, damn you! I've done nothing to deserve being spattered with filth like this."

"Go ahead! Clobber me! The mother of your four daughters — you want to ditch me! I'm not fresh and tasty like her. All right, beat me to death, then you can take a new wife."

Peppery butted his chest with her head, ramming him against the wall. Unable to shove her away, Mangeng quivered with fury, his eyes flashing fire.

"Heaven strike you dead! Hiding loot for your fancy woman! Do you want this family or not? What did the team leader say at yesterday's meeting? Do you want to land me and the kids in trouble too? You hand in that money, or you'll be the death of us all! ... Heavens, she's stolen your heart away! You'd wrap her sweat rag round your neck! I'll report you to the work team, see if I don't, and get them to send militia here to search!"

Thwack! Peppery was knocked to the ground. Beside himself, Mangeng had hit her so hard that she lay limply in one corner. For fear she would get up and make a fresh scene, he pinned her down with his knee.

"Will you stop bitching? Raising such a row at this hour of the night! Who wears the pants in this family, eh? Want me to knock you dead? Anyway I've nothing to live for."

In desperation Mangeng punched his own head.

Peppery lay on the floor, blood oozing from her lips, her nose black and swollen. But at least she was frightened into keeping quiet.

By now the four children had woken and run in crying.

Their daughters' cries acted like some magic cure for madness. Mangeng at once let his wife go. She scrambled up and grabbed for some clothes, ashamed to let the little girls see her half-naked.

Dogs were barking outside. Their neighbours had been aroused. They came over now to make peace. Tapping on the windows and doors, they called, "Secretary! Sister-in-law!"

After this intervention the storm subsided. They shut their door and went back to bed again. Peppery ignored her husband, turning her face to the wall. She had stopped crying, but Mangeng sobbed to himself:

"Heavens . . . how are we to get by! . . . These people are like mad dogs out for blood. They've no conscience, they've hardened their hearts. Poor thing . . . I never let you down, did what I thought right . . . you can't treat people like cattle. . . . But I doubt if I can get by in this movement myself. . . . If you don't trample on others they trample on you — that's the only way to get on nowadays. , , ,"

There is something fearful about a grown man
weeping. This was the first time in his thirty-odd years
that Mangeng had sobbed like this. His wife was
aghast. But her resentment still rankled. When she
heard him sobbing more and more bitterly, she sat up to
reason with him. However big a fool he'd made of
himself, he was still her man.

"What's the idea! You knock me down and trample
on me as if I were one of the Five Categories — isn't
that enough to work off your hatred? Have you no
conscience? However ugly or low-class I am, I'm your
wife who's slaved for you, borne you six children. I'm
your four daughters' ma — yet you knock me down,
give me black eyes . . . kneel on my breast. . . . Oh, why
ever was I born? Life isn't worth living!"

She had meant to talk him round, but instead her
resentment surfaced again, making her feel so sorry for
herself that now she too began sobbing. She pinched
Mangeng's shoulder hard.

"A dog must have eaten your conscience. . . . I flew
off the handle too, I shouldn't have cursed you. You
have no feeling for me, none at all . . . but I feel for
you, you wretch. . . . You ought to know, when I swear
at you I love you. . . . If you've no feeling for your ugly
wife, you ought to have some for our sweet little
girls. . . ." This outburst had been punctuated by sobs.

Mangeng's heart softened. Tears pouring down his
cheeks, he took his wife in his arms. Yes, this woman,
these four children and this home were his. He and his
wife had worked hard for eight years like magpies
building their nest twig by twig.

Peppery's heart softened too. She knelt in front of
her husband, placing his hands on her heart.

"Mangeng, you take my advice. . . . You're Party secretary, you understand the policy in this movement, what's meant by a struggle to the death. . . . We mustn't die, we must live on. . . . You can't wrap fire in paper — the truth will out. You mustn't keep that money. . . . Remember Land Reform, when those people who hid gold and silver for the landlords were beaten half to death and had to wear tall hats. . . . Turn it in to the work team. If you don't, someone else will blab. . . . It's not as if we're selling her out . . . we aren't. She has only herself to blame. In our new society, everybody should get rich together or be poor together, instead of trying to feather their own nests the way she has. . . ."

Mangeng held his wife close. He was still weeping inwardly. He seemed to have said goodbye to his original self, for that old Mangeng would never have passed the test of this "life and death" struggle.

## Manager Gu

A notice came down from the Organization Department of the county committee and the County Grain Bureau: "As Manager Gu Yanshan of Hibiscus Grain Depot has lost his class stand and stolen state grain to sell, his case is extremely serious; he must be suspended from his post at once to make a self-examination and write a confession." This notice was read out by the work team at a meeting of all members of the grain depot except for Gu Yanshan. This was a real bolt from the blue. Gu, confined to his bedroom upstairs, lost all freedom of action. The work team appointed two activists to guard his door day and night for fear, or so they said, that he might commit suicide. At first he could not believe his own ears or eyes but thought he was having a ridiculous nightmare. It couldn't be true! It was like a play or film produced by a man who had never been near the front, never been to a village — you could see at a glance how bogus the whole thing was. Once he had seen a war film in which the instructor stood facing the enemy line and yelled, "Comrades, for motherland and people, for all our oppressed class brothers throughout the world, charge!" Heavens, who had time to speechify on a battlefield? Presenting yourself as a target! How bogus, ridiculous and maddening. But this order to him to stop work and write a confession was genuine. He wasn't deaf or blind, he wasn't dreaming. And so this "soldier from the north", known to all Hibiscus for his good temper and decency, was roused from his stupefaction. He blew his top, pounded the table, chairs and partition.

"Work team!" he bellowed. "Who do you think you are! You've sent in false reports to the county committee! Li Guoxiang, you creep, at last you've torn off your mask! To my face you call me old comrade, old revolutionary, then suddenly you stab me in the back. In the war years we launched surprise attacks against the Japs and Old Chiang; but you, you use this tactic against comrades. . . . While we fought tunnel warfare, under fire, you were still wetting your nappies! To win New China, blood streamed and corpses piled up, yet now you're attacking people right and left, not letting anybody live in peace. . . ."

Gu Yanshan tugged and kicked at the door, but it was padlocked outside — no doubt because his attitude was so bad. The two activists ignored him, smoking and chatting as they stood guard with their guns. Maybe guns that Old Gu and his comrades-in-arms had captured from the Japanese.

"Hey, you watch-dogs! Open up! Open the door. I'll teach you to take aim and fire.... Why lock me in? What sort of lock-up is this? If I'm to go to prison I'll go to the county, I refuse to stay in this private lock-up of yours!"

No one paid any attention. They were letting him off lightly by not handcuffing him. Struggle is ruthless, with no room for such bourgeois weaknesses as human-kindness. Eventually he tired, his throat hoarse and dry. Then, having drunk a cup of icy water, he flopped down with his back against the door and dozed off. He woke up in the middle of the night, freezing. It was too dark to see a thing. He groped his way to the bed to wrap a blanket round himself, then paced to and fro like a besieged or captured general. His mind seemed clear enough now to start assessing what had happened. At once he felt rather remorseful. How disgraceful for a Communist, a veteran soldier, to carry on like an old woman, pounding the door and disturbing the whole street because of a bit of injustice. Gu Yanshan, Gu Yanshan, it's twenty years since you joined the revolution, joined the Party — can't you stand a little test? You think in peace-time everything is plain sailing, with never a cloud in the sky, never a storm? You were only a platoon leader when you were demobbed to work here, a piddling little cadre.... Then some notions which he normally suppressed, being afraid to admit them, flashed to his mind. You served in the North China Field Army under Commander Peng Dehuai.

Well, Commander Peng, one of the founders of the state, just because he spoke up for the people in '59 in Lushan and came out against everybody smelting steel and eating in communal canteens, was sacked from his post, stripped of his uniform and labelled a rightist opportunist. Everyone knew that was unjust, it was wrong to criticize and struggle against him — the last thing the people wanted. Then our country had three hard years, stopped the nationwide smelting of steel, stopped sending up boastful sputniks, stopped eating in communal canteens, taking his advice after all. . . . But what was this present movement? The people had just caught their breath, production was just picking up, life improving a bit, yet here they were settling scores for the relaxation of policies during the hard years, which they now called a "rightist deviation". They were tearing down the bridge after crossing the river, turning against their friends. . . . Commander Peng, Gu Yanshan is nobody compared with you. The manager of a grain depot in a small town, an ordinary "soldier from the north", and they've just made me stop working to think over my mistakes. They haven't clapped me in prison or handcuffed me. How fantastic, a Communist in a Party prison! What rubbish. . . . Of course Gu knew this way of thinking was very, very dangerous. If people found out he'd be for it, he'd really land up in gaol.

Gu Yanshan's morale fluctuated and he kept changing his mind. He could make no sense of this struggle in which he was involved. Commander Peng, actuated by a sense of justice, had spoken out for the people. When had he, Gu Yanshan, ever thought about or discussed the government? He wasn't up to that, not by a long chalk. He had always been loyal, doing what the Party said. He was just a decent fellow in the Wuling Mountains, an ordinary, insignificant nobody.... How come this revolutionary struggle had to burst out in their own ranks and start by annihilating its own fighters? A "life-and-death" struggle, how appallingly grim! Had he really let the Party and revolution down? "Stolen state grain to sell" — maybe that referred to the sixty pounds of seconds he'd sold to Sister Hibiscus for her beancurd.... What a fool he was! This was as clear as day to everyone in town, but it had taken him three days to figure this out.

After grasping this he felt easier in his mind. It wasn't as serious as the work team or the notice from the county made out. These last few years plenty of organizations as well as individuals had bought seconds from the grain depot to feed pigs, poultry or rabbits. Of course, maybe he shouldn't have supplied Hu Yuyin with any.... Hell, what gave him that idea?... Honestly, though no womanizer and known by the whole town for his decency, he had taken a fancy to Yuyin, to her smiling face and big eyes with such black pupils and clear whites. He liked to hear her voice. When he sat by her beancurd stall he felt at home. Was that a crime? Deprived of a woman's warmth, couldn't he have a warm place in his heart for a woman? This was nothing immoral, didn't affect her marriage; so he had decided to help Sister Hibiscus. Did those rice seconds undergo some qualitative change when made into beancurd? Was that what made this so wrong?

Little by little he calmed down. He knew he would be detained upstairs for a couple of months to "think over his mistakes", watched even when he peed. It was hard to get through the time. Previously, first thing in the morning, he had swept the street in front of the grain depot, joking with the commune members off to the fields, hugging every child with a satchel. In the evening he had the habit of strolling down the street to pass the time, stopping at the door of some shop for a chat. Sometimes he would be dragged in to drink a cup of sweet-potato liquor and eat some fried peanuts, and they would have a good yarn about past and present.... Now he was denied these diversions. The street was so near yet so far!

Five days after Gu was suspended to make a self-examination, Li Guoxiang came upstairs to explain the policy to him.

"Been feeling rather tense these days, Old Gu?" she asked sweetly. "Ah, we respected you as an old comrade and wanted to learn from you, not realising how serious your problem was. The county committee may be using it as an example in this movement!" Gu always felt that her golden voice was wasted in Hibiscus and she ought to have been an announcer in the county broadcasting station.

He nodded coolly at her. His attitude to the team leader was a mixture of contempt, admiration and pity. But now, representing the county committee, she held the fate of Hibiscus in her hands, including his own fate. The higher-ups respected her for her ability. At big meetings or small or when chatting, phrases like "Marxism-Leninism", "class struggle" and "the Four Clean-ups" kept pouring from her lips. She could talk for hours at a stretch without drinking a drop of water or ever once coughing, as if she had been to a college to learn revolutionary terminology.

"Well? What have you been thinking these days? No matter how serious the problem, if you make a clean breast of it to the Party it won't be hard to clear up. And as far as I'm concerned, the earlier you take this bath, the earlier you can 'come downstairs' and join the revolutionary masses in this great movement to re-educate our Party members and cadres, and to reorganize our class contingents." To show her sincerity and touch this "soldier from the north", Li Guoxiang added, "See, I made a point of talking to you alone, without the other members of the work team. At least I have no prejudice against you."

Gu Yanshan, untouched by her sincerity, shot her a glance which seemed to imply: You can say whatever you like, don't expect me to agree.

Apparently sensing his antagonism, she decided to needle him. She produced her notebook and leafed through it slowly till she reached a certain page. Her expression sterner, she said formally:

"Listen, Gu Yanshan, to the figures in this account. The work team has established that in the two years and nine months since the second half of 1961, Hibiscus has had six markets a month, making one hundred and ninety-eight in all. Before each, you sold sixty pounds of rice to the pedlar Hu Yuyin, a new bourgeois element, to make beancurd. That totals 11,880 pounds of rice — right?"

"Over ten thousand pounds!" Sure enough, Gu sprang to his feet as if struck by lightning. He had never figured this out.

"A sizeable amount, eh?" Her eyes glinted. She seemed to be gloating: See, I goad you once and up you jump. You're easy to handle.

"Those were seconds, not the good rice from the state storehouse," protested Old Gu loudly and indignantly.

"Never mind that. As manager of the grain depot you issued ten thousand pounds, didn't you? Did you grow that rice? Wasn't it from the state storehouse? Did you report this to the county? Who gave you so much authority?" Li Guoxiang sat there motionless as she fired off these questions.

"Seconds are seconds, rice is rice. I sold it to her at the official price, to other units and individuals too. You can check our accounts. Didn't make a cent extra profit."

"So clean you didn't make a cent? Well, maybe. But a bachelor has his way of being paid. . . ." she prompted him. She was watching him with secret pleasure like a hunter watching a goat fall into his trap. "Surely you don't need the work team to remind you."

"What way has a bachelor of being paid?"

"That beancurd pedlar's the beauty of Hibiscus. Her flesh is so soft and white!"

"What a thing for a woman to say!"

"Don't give me that talk. What cat doesn't like salted fish? It's not too late yet for you to come clean. When did your relationship start? This is up her street, wasn't her mother a prostitute?"

"You think we had an affair?" Gu, his eyes nearly popping out, fell back two paces.

"Well?" Li Guoxiang tilted her head coquettishly.

"Team Leader Li! How could I have it off with her? How could I?" The veins on Gu's forehead stood out, as he backed against the wall. "Li Guoxiang! Call in your colleagues, and I'll take off my pants to show them. . . . Hell, that was a slip of the tongue. . . ."

"Gu Yanshan, you hoodlum!" She rapped the desk and stood up, as if she had lost patience. Eyes dilated, eyebrows raised, she looked furious. "Taking such liberties with me! An old bachelor! So you want to take off your pants. I'll call the whole town to a meeting and let you expose yourself to everyone! Insulting the work team! Remember who you are!"

"I, I forgot myself, you pushed me so hard. . . . I take that back. . . ." Old Gu was an honest fellow with little experience of struggle, so that when anyone had a handle against him he quickly backed down. He covered his face with his hands. "I've done other wrong things, but this I can't do. I'm impotent, dammit. . . ."

"Tell the truth, that's better." She was amazed and intrigued by his disclosure, delighted at having won a moral victory over him. "Sit down, Old Gu. Let's both sit down. Keep calm. I haven't lost my temper with you. You've done wrong, so how can you take that attitude? Our work team sticks to the Party policy, penalizing cadres to make them mend their ways, curing illness to save the patient. The only people we attack mercilessly are those dead against the movement. . . ."

With that she went back to the desk and sat down. Old Gu also went back to his seat. He felt limp and utterly wretched.

At this point the two activists poked their heads round the door, but Li Guoxiang waved them away.

"To repeat what I said before, Old Gu. You can clear everything up with the work team, and I can tell the county committee I'll be responsible for you." She was chatting pleasantly again in a fresh bout of psychological warfare, meaning to strike while the iron was hot so as to crush once for all this popular leading figure in Hibiscus. "Your problem goes far beyond this, and may be much more serious than we think. Even if you've not had an affair with Hu Yuyin, you're involved with her financially and ideologically. You used ten thousand pounds of seconds — if they were seconds — to help her give up farming and go in for capitalist-style trading. Hers is the biggest newly rich family in all Hibiscus. She's not a simple woman. What's her relationship to Li Mangeng? They call themselves brother and sister, but Li Mangeng isn't impotent like you, is he? You know, Hu Yuyin for all her fine looks is barren. Li Mangeng has given her political protection to make huge profits all this time in Hibiscus. And what's the relationship between him and Qin Shutian? Between Qin Shutian and Hu Yuyin? Between her and that tax officer from a bureaucrat landlord family? We've checked up that the tax-office only collected a dollar's tax from Hu Yuyin for each market, though her turnover was more than three hundred yuan. What does that mean? So for a long time you people, inside and outside the Party, have actually been in cahoots, making use of each other and ganging up together to run Hibiscus. In fact, you're a clique."

Here Li Guoxiang paused.

Gu's forehead was beaded with sweat. "Clique! What clique! That's a dirty lie, a frame-up."

"What, afraid? You can't deny it." Li Guoxiang raised her voice and spoke sternly. "Of course, if you all admit it and make a clean breast, we may not classify you as a clique. Three feet of ice isn't formed overnight! Last year some of the revolutionary masses reported you to the county committee. . . . The work team can recommend not dealing with you like a clique

— but that depends largely on your own attitude. Hu Yuyin's attitude is bad, she's run away in fright. But we've arrested her husband Li Guigui for questioning.... Old Gu, you're known in town as a good sort, a peace-maker; people all look up to you, so you'd better give the lead while the way's still open. Otherwise the consequences will be serious...."

How well-meaning she sounded, showing such great forbearance.

"Heavens, I'll stake my head on it, there's no clique in Hibiscus."

Gu Yanshan seemed suddenly to have aged ten years. His whole body was wet with cold sweat.


## The Young Widow

Yuyin stayed for two months with Guigui's distant relatives in Xiuzhou, waiting for the trouble in Hibiscus to blow over. "Keep out of harm's way" was the common people's motto for coping with disaster. However, "A monk can run away, but not a monastery," and certain disasters are unavoidable. Especially as in the new society each policy prevailed throughout the country, and no matter how far you fled you could be recalled by telephone or telegram.

For two months Yuyin had been thinking day and night of her "monastery" in Hibiscus. She had received one encouraging letter from Guigui, telling her that the movement was in full swing there and all the Five Categories had been rounded up and harangued, then paraded in front of a demonstration of the townsfolk. All the former cadres had disappeared, everything was now run by the work team. The tax-officer from a bureaucrat landlord family had been criticized and struggled against. The militia had raided several households, and his cleaver had been confiscated. So much the better, it was a lethal weapon. . . . It was said that in this movement people were going to be reclassified. He ended up by insisting that she should stay away, and on no account write.

How useless Guigui was, not saying a word about his situation apart from the confiscation of his cleaver. Yuyin could only guess what was happening. He said the cadres had disappeared — did that mean Manager Gu and Brother Mangeng? Which houses had been raided? Their new storeyed building? In the reclassification would they be given a new class status? . . . Oh, Guigui, how thoughtless of you not to write more clearly. That was the only letter she had from him. Had Guigui been arrested? The more she speculated, the more her heart misgave her. She was like a hen cooped up after a guest's arrival, conscious of some impending calamity. Just what calamity, no one had told her. Would she be put in the Five Categories, the scum of the earth, those ragged, grimy devils who were pelted with pebbles and clods by schoolchildren, hauled out in each movement or struggle for the revolutionary masses to spit at, curse and beat? . . .

Heavens, if she sank so low, how could she live on? Impossible! She had never done anything wrong, never said anything reactionary or sworn at the cadres. To her Manager Gu and Brother Mangeng had seemed like her own family. How could a beancurd pedlar hate the new society which had done her no harm? After Liberation there were no more bandits or kidnappers, men no longer gambled, played cards or took concubines; everyone could sleep soundly at night. It was good, the new society. If not for it, a poor girl with her looks would long ago have been kidnapped and carried off to some brothel. . . . No, it was the Five Categories who were bad, black-hearted wretches. How could she be lumped together with such scum?

At this time word went round the county town of Xiuzhou that a work team would be coming to launch another movement like land reform. Indeed, people had called to ask her relatives, "Where is this sister-in-law from? What's her class? How long has she been staying here? Has she a letter vouching for her from her commune?" She had too much tact, too much self-respect to outstay her welcome and involve her hosts. "There is no escaping disaster." She decided to ignore Guigui's advice and go back to Hibiscus. Indeed, she should have realized earlier that now of all times she ought to be with her husband, ought to share whatever fate was in store for them. She wanted to be buried in the same grave as Guigui. It's too bad of you, Yuyin! How cruel of you to neglect him for two whole months. . . . Hurry now! Hurry!

She walked from dawn till dusk, urging herself, "Hurry, hurry!" All she was carrying was a brown satchel with a change of clothes and a torch. She had two snacks on the way, one of rice fried with eggs, the other of two bowls of beancurd. Too much soda in the beancurd had made it rather yellow. It wasn't as white and soft as hers, nor served with as much oil and fla-vouring. And the white-aproned woman attendant be-haved as if she were dishing out charity, not laughing and joking with her customers. Yuyin's customers, when they put down their bowls to leave, would say, "I'm off now, sister. See you at the next market." "So long then. Keep out of mischief on the way, your wife's watching out for you."

She reached Hibiscus at nightfall.

"Who's there?" A man with a gun stepped out of the darkness. She knew him, he was a young fellow from the rice mill. When she had gone to the grain depot to buy seconds, powdered with white from head to foot he used to beg jokingly:

"Elder sister, be my go-between. A bachelor's ilfe is hard."

"What kind of wife do you want?"

"One as white and pretty as you, with big eyes and arched eyebrows."

"You wretch! I'll find you a bitch."

"I want one with a willowy waist and high breasts like yours."

"Get away with you, you clod. . . . I'll call your Manager Gu."

"How cruel you are, sister!"

"Scram! Your parents died too soon to teach you manners."

Well, it seemed the movement was still going on in Hibiscus, so men stood guard at night and even this young rascal could carry a gun.

"It's you, eh? Come back on your own?" He recognized her, but his harsh voice was like the crack of a whip. Then, ignoring her, he walked aside with his gun. Normally he would have clowned and cracked crude jokes.

"Come back on your own?" Her heart missed a beat. What did that mean? If she hadn't come, would they

have sent to arrest her? She virtually ran into the flagstone street. The shutters were up on the shops, but she
couldn't make out what the slogans which covered them
were. In front of her inn she stumbled and nearly
fell. On the door was the old brass padlock, so Guigui
was out. The padlock at least was familiar, it was the
one left by her dad and mum. She took a deep breath.
But what of the new storeyed building next door? What
were those strips of white paper on the gate? Two of
them formed a cross. So evidently their house hadn't
simply been raided, it had been sealed up. She fumbled
in her satchel for her torch and shone it on the red
gate. On it was nailed a notice: Exhibition of the Class
Struggle in Hibiscus. So her house had been taken over
as an exhibition hall? Guigui hadn't said a word about
this in his letter. . . . Guigui, you good-for-nothing, where
have you got to at this hour of the night? Your wife's
back, but instead of coming to meet her you leave the
gate locked.

She knew it was no use searching for Guigui, she'd
get no sense out of him. She decided to go and see
Manager Gu Yanshan. He was a true friend, fair-mind-
ed, glad to help people. The only old revolutionary in
town, he had prestige and his words carried weight. . . .
She glided noiselessly down the flagstone street, as if
about to take flight. The grain depot's front gate was
locked but the small side gate was open. When the
gateman saw her he recoiled as if at the sight of a
ghost. . . . Why was that? In the past people meeting
her in the street, the men especially, had always smiled
at her. . . .

"Can you tell me, uncle, if Manager Gu is in?" She

ignored his strange look in her eagerness to find Old Gu.

"Woman Hu, are you looking for Old Gu?" The gatekeeper turned to peer inside, then peeked out at the road. Seeing no one about he said gruffly, "It's no use looking for Old Gu, you've got him into big trouble. He's said to have stolen ten thousand pounds of state grain and sold it to encourage capitalism. . . . He's too closely watched day and night to even find a belt to hang himself, poor sod. . . ."

Yuyin's heart contracted. . . . What, Old Gu under house arrest . . . she could never have dreamed it. To her Old Gu represented the new society, the government, the Party. But now he was locked up. What could such a decent, kindly man have done wrong? Men like him had shed their blood to win New China, how could they be against the new regime?

She went back to the flagstone street. Looking up she saw that the light was still on in Manager Gu's room upstairs. She stared at it unblinkingly. Was Old Gu writing confessions under the lamp, or trying to think of a way to outwit his guards and commit suicide? He mustn't do that. Old Gu, don't take it so hard, someone must have thrown dirt at you. All the people of Hibiscus can vouch for you to the county and the province. We'll send in a petition. Every man, woman and child in town knows that you've never done anything wrong, you're such a decent sort. For a moment Yuyin forgot her own fearful predicament in her indignation and concern for Old Gu.

Ah, now she remembered, over three months ago Li Guoxiang the head of the work team had gone to her new storeyed house and sat upstairs in the newly furnished room to do some reckoning for her. According to her, in two years and nine months she'd made over six thousand yuan from selling beancurd, and someone had supplied her with ten thousand pounds of rice.... That must be why Old Gu was being kept a prisoner. Well, she was the one to blame, the one who had made money — why blame Old Gu? And some of the proceeds from her sale of beancurd were in Brother Mangeng's keeping.

She must find Brother Mangeng. Most likely he was still in charge of Hibiscus. He'd acknowledged her as his sister, so he would protect her. He was even closer to her than a real brother.... Yuyin made off at a run. For all her confusion she wasn't completely at sea. And her steps were so light and noiseless she seemed to be flying.... Ah, Brother Mangeng, you couldn't marry me . . . a Party member couldn't take a wife like me . . . but you held me in your arms and kissed me on the wharf. Held me so tight that it hurt, and swore to look after me as long as you lived.... Brother Mangeng, that stone slab on the wharf is still there.... I know you'll look after me. Brother Mangeng, you must save me, save your sister....

She had no idea how she ferried across the river or climbed the opposite bank.... She knocked at Mangeng's gate. She had seldom been into his house but she knew it well. Hefty Peppery came out to open the door. But she was taken aback when she saw her. The women in town had always stared at her with envious admiration. Women tended to be jealous. But how was it that now everyone in town, men and women, old and young, looked at her as if she were a ghost or jinx?

"Is Brother Mangeng at home?" she asked. Never mind his wife's expression, she must find the man who loved her and had promised to protect her.

"Please don't ever come looking for him again! You nearly did for him, for our whole family. . . . The kids and I nearly got tarred with the same brush. . . . Now the higher-ups have sent him to the county town to make a self-examination and study. Off he went with his bedding-roll. . . . I can tell you, someone let on about that one thousand five hundred yuan you gave him, and he handed it over to the work team. . . ."

"Oh . . . men. . . . Heavens, how can men be so heartless. . . ."

Yuyin felt deafened and dizzy, as if after a clap of thunder. She staggered and nearly fell.

"Men? That man of yours had a nerve! Threatened to kill the work team head. He's in the graveyard now!"

With that Peppery slammed the gate shut as if shooing away a beggar. A big, solid gate it was.

Yuyin wanted to sink into the ground. . . . But she couldn't lie at their gate like a real beggar. She bore up, surprised by her own stamina, then walked off, her steps light and noiseless, as if about to take flight.

"Where are you, Guigui? Peppery said you wanted to kill the work team head, but you never would — you haven't the guts. If you meet a shaggy dog or a cow with a crooked horn, you dodge in fright. . . . No, you'd never do such a thing. Guigui, you're the only dear one I have left in the whole world. Why hide yourself away in the graveyard? What are you up to, you idiot? That's where all the townsfolk are buried and no one dares to go there even by daylight, so why is a scaredy-cat like you skulking there in the dark?"

Her thoughts were in a whirl ... yet suddenly she had a premonition. Oh, Guigui, dear Guigui, don't tell me you've ... no, you couldn't. Surely you must have waited to see me again. ...

She was crying aloud as she raced along the rough track, running as fast as her legs would carry her, yet not falling. What a fool she was, crying and shouting, so worked up over nothing. Isn't that Guigui? He's come ... yes, it's Guigui, my Guigui! ...

When Guigui was just twenty-two, Yuyin just eighteen, an old butcher had acted as their go-between. The first time she set eyes on him he was tall and lean, with fine features and a ruddy face, so shy that he wanted to hide behind the door. ... Her dad and mum had said: His trade is butchering, good! To start with she'd been silly enough to compare him with Brother Mangeng, and of course Guigui didn't measure up to him. So, resenting this, Yuyin had cold-shouldered him. She hung her head, pouting, inwardly cursing his gall. But Guigui was an honest fellow. Without so much as a murmur he had come to the inn every day to fetch them water, chop firewood and sweep the floor. He mended the roof when it leaked, and washed their mosquito nets and quilts in the river. Every day he came to help out quickly and efficiently with the chores, then took himself off, not letting her parents persuade him to stay for a meal or even a drink of tea. ... The neighbours said Innkeeper Hu must have done good deeds in an earlier life to have found himself such an honest son-in-law. They said Yuyin was in luck, getting such a husband to come and live in her home. Most likely she could leave all the housework to him and live a pampered life. . . . Oddly enough, the more she disliked this Guigui. the more highly everybody spoke of him. And he seemed to be bursting with energy just to impress her. Later on, like a busy beaver, he even took to washing her clothes, shoes and stockings on the sly. All right, wash them if you want to! You can wash them all your life if you're so hard-working. I'll pretend not to see and pay no attention to you.

For half a year or so her attitude to him had been one of guarded neutrality. But then by degrees, devil take it, it dawned on Yuyin that Guigui was handsome, good-tempered and well-mannered. She took a liking to him, coming to appreciate his good qualities. So it irked her if he happened not to come to the inn for a day, and she would keep going to the gate to look out for him. . . . That pleased her dad and mum and made their neighbours exchange significant smiles. Why? Because Guigui had taken Mangeng's place in her heart. Besides, Mangeng was married now to a woman as strong as he was, an amazon capable of killing a tiger. Why shouldn't Guigui compare favourably with him? Guigui was her man, her husband. There was nothing wrong with him. He was hard-working, handy, kindly and soft-spoken. They had a magnificent, truly stylish wedding at which actresses lovely as fairies from the county song-and-dance ensemble performed and sang wedding songs all evening. Later some of the older women in Hibiscus said that not even the rich men for a hundred *li* around had ever put on such an impressive wedding. . . .

Gusts of wind flattened the grass and bent the trees as Yuyin rushed recklessly forward. . . .

Guigui was beside her, talking to her and keeping her company.... Do you remember, Guigui? On our wedding night those lovely actresses pushed us into the bridal chamber, then went away. We were both tired out after all that dancing and singing. You were red in the face, you fool, hanging your head, afraid even to glance at me. You went to bed without daring to get undressed. I didn't know whether to laugh or to be angry. Why, you were as bashful as a bride.... Did you think I wasn't shy? You were shyer than I was, you fool. I suddenly felt you were more like my younger brother than my husband. (My, at that time the word "husband" made my cheeks burn, my heart beat fast.) I didn't think a man like you would swear at me or be unkind and beat me. I thought you'd do what I wanted.... That night we both slept in our clothes, didn't touch each other. How laughable it seems now. The next morning you got up before it was light to fetch water, get the breakfast and sweep up the shells of melon seeds and peanuts littering the hall. I didn't know that, I was still sound asleep. Oh, Guigui, I'm still rather spoilt, first by my dad and mum, and then by you....

"Yes, Guigui, I love being spoilt by you, but you were such a nincompoop of a bridegroom, you were even more bashful than I was — remember? The second evening, a lantern-slide team came to town. We had no films in those days but used to watch lantern-slides once a month, right? Before Liberation all we had were shadow plays and lanterns. I remember that lantern-slide showed *Young Erhei's Marriage*. The young couple were really good-looking. Because they didn't want their parents to arrange their marriages for them, they met at night in a wood, and thugs tied them up and

took them to the district government. As we watched
I snuggled up to you. How feudal that was, marriages
arranged by go-betweens, and the village cadres tying
young people up. How lucky we were to have been
born in the new society, with no more feudalism, able
to sit together, a man and a girl, without anyone tying
us up. It was very dark there that night, with not a star
in the sky. I remember, while you watched, you put
your arm round my waist. Then you whipped it away
as if you were afraid of being scalded, till I grabbed
it and gently slapped you. Why not put your arm around
me? I was your wife, you were my husband, not any
hooligan. . . . After that you didn't let go. . . .

"Guigui, Guigui! How well we always get on together, because you always do whatever I want. You call
me your commander, your empress. Where did you
pick up such silly names? From watching a few old
operas and new plays? And I've been good to you too,
never throwing tantrums. All those years we've never
flared up at each other. Not that it didn't upset us being
married seven years without having a baby. . . . How
we longed for a baby, Guigui! Without one, we always
felt there was something missing, no matter how fond
we were of one another — it seemed as if our marriage
wasn't for keeps. A baby, flesh of our flesh, would
have kept us together all our lives. . . . Because of this
I often wept behind your back and you often sighed in
secret. Actually we each knew how the other felt, but
both pretended not to. . . . Later we squabbled over
this, but not loudly enough for the neighbours to
overhear. In fact you didn't blame me, I blamed
myself. . . . Later I had the superstitious notion that it
was because we doted so on each other that we couldn't

ever have children. We should squabble and scold
each other like other couples. . . . Oh, Guigui! Why
don't you say anything? You keep frowning, what's
upset you? Do you blame me for selling beancurd, for
building that new storeyed house which landed us in
trouble? We quarrelled over that, and I stabbed you
with my chopsticks because you wanted to sell it at a
loss. . . ."

Yuyin sped on through the night, beside herself, her
thoughts wandering. All around was dark and she felt
dazed. She couldn't remember who had ferried her
across the river on her way back. She ran on, as if to
catch up with someone ahead. "Guigui, wait for me!
Don't be unkind! Wait for me!" she cried. "I've a
whole lot more to tell you. I want your advice on something very important. . . ."

Someone seemed to be running after her with pounding footsteps. A ghost or a man? She couldn't be
bothered to look in her impatience to catch up with her
husband. Probably it was a man, ghosts were said to
make no sound. Why should anyone chase her? She had
no possessions, nothing but the tail-end of her life. Did
they have to criticize her, struggle against her, tie her
up? I want to be with Guigui, with my Guigui. . . . If
you catch me and tie me up, I shall bite through the rope
. . . .

At last she climbed up to the graveyard. People said
this place was haunted, but she was not afraid. There
were thousands of grave mounds here, where from way
back whole generations of townsfolk had been buried.
They had all found their final resting-place here, the
good spirits, the ghosts of those unjustly killed, old and

young, good and evil, men and women, whether bound for heaven or hell.

"Guigui! Where are you? Where are you?"

It was too dark to make out which of the grave mounds was new or old.

"Guigui! Where are you? Answer me! Your wife's coming to see you! . . ."

Her shrill mournful cries hung in the air, overriding all other sounds, like green will-o'-the-wisps in the darkness, and floating out over the desolate graveyard. She rushed wildly over the uneven ground. On the road she had never once stumbled, but here she kept falling down, hardly able to scramble up again, as if she would sleep here among the graves for ever.

"Sister Hibiscus! Stop calling, stop looking for him. Brother Guigui can't answer you."

After a while someone helped her to her feet.

"Who are you? Who are you?"

"Who am I? Don't you know my voice?"

"Are you a ghost?"

"What should I say? Sometimes a ghost, sometimes a man."

"You. . . ."

"I'm Qin Shutian, Crazy Qin."

"One of the Five Categories! Scram! Leave me alone!"

"I only want to help you, Sister Hibiscus. You simply mustn't take this too much to heart. You must take care of yourself, you've still years to live. . . ."

"I don't want you here, don't want your pity. Pitch dark it is, and you're a bad lot, a Rightist. . . ."

"Sister . . . Li Guigui was classified as a new rich peasant. That makes you. . . ."

"You're lying! What new rich peasant?"

"It's the truth I'm telling you. . . ."

"Ha, ha, so I'm the wife of a new rich peasant! A beancurd pedlar the wife of a new rich peasant! Are you trying to scare me, you wretch?"

"I'm not, I'm telling the truth, not making this up."

"The truth?"

"Tortoises don't make fun of turtles, they're all in the mud. In the same fix."

"Heavens, a rich peasant's wife. . . . This is all your doing, you wretch. . . . When we married you brought all those tramps to oppose feudalism by singing wedding songs. You spoilt my luck, that was the ruin of us. . . ." Yuyin broke down and sobbed. "Why did you have to collect those songs? Why oppose feudalism? You ruined yourself for life, and as if that wasn't enough you ruined Guigui and me. . . ."

> Candles cast a ghostly light,
> Wax tears from them seeping:
> When the candles go out the tears dry,
> But the girl is hoarse from weeping.
> Candles cast a ghostly light
> As we sing at her wedding;
> We sing of heart-rending grief,
> Of all the tears she's shedding.

Crazy Qin was really crazy. He sat on a grave mound singing this song he had written years ago for that poisonous dance-drama of his *Wedding Songs*.

# Part 3
# The Nature of Men and Devils
## (1969)

## New Customs and Bad Ways

BY the end of the Four Clean-ups Movement Hibiscus,
once a "black lair of capitalism", had changed into a
"fortress of socialism". This metamorphosis first
manifested itself in the narrow flagstone street. The
shops on both sides, originally of dark timber, now
had the lower halves of their walls white-washed
and given a scarlet border. Every other shop
bore a slogan in standard script "Promote What Is
Proletarian and Liquidate What Is Bourgeois", "In
Agriculture Learn from Dazhai", "Defend the Fruits
of the Four Clean-ups", "Grasp Class Struggle and All
Problems Can Be Solved". Every gate was painted
with couplets identical in size and in identical calligraphy: "Take the Dazhai Road," "Raise the Red
Banner of Dazhai." So the whole street had uniformity
with red slogans and couplets on white. In the past,
on fine days bamboo poles had been fixed up between
opposite upstairs windows to dry or air clothes and
bedding, bright red and green, which hung there like
countless flags adding colour to Hibiscus. Now to
dignify the street these were done away with. At festi-

vals, or when higher-ups came on a tour of inspection, or other brigades came to learn from their experience, each family had to hang a red flag from its attic over the street. These hung limp if there was no wind, but fluttered triumphantly in a breeze. A rule was also made that no dogs, poultry, rabbits or bees could be kept, in the interests of sanitation. However, each household was allowed three hens. There was no explicit rule about the use to which these hens should be put: most likely the money fetched by their eggs was spent on salt and oil, or a couple of eggs were poached for the cadres who came down to the county and boarded with different families. Street stalls were strictly forbidden; pedlars had to till the land and give up trading.

So the town's appearance was revolutionized. And an even more thoroughgoing revolution took place in the relations between the townsfolk. A system of public security was instituted: visitors had to register, people making a trip had to ask for leave, and in the evenings militiamen patrolled the town. At both ends and in the centre of the street there were three "impeachment boxes", and no action could be taken against those who wrote anonymous letters accusing their neighbours. Failure to report an offence was itself a crime, while informing on others was laudable and would be set down to your credit in your file; in addition to which you would be commended and rewarded. These boxes were locked and unlocked at regular intervals by the man in charge. The results of this system were spectacular. As soon as darkness fell every household bolted its gate and turned in early to save lamp oil, so the whole town was quiet. Even in the daytime neighbours stopped calling on each other, to avoid making off-colour remarks which might be reported and land them in trouble. The townsfolk had liked to be neighbourly and treat each other to snacks, but now that bourgeois humanism was under fire, they pricked up their ears and strained their eyes to keep close watch on each other. Whereas their motto had been "each for all and all for each", they were now on their guard against everybody else.

Besides, class alignments had been clarified. After countless meetings large and small and various political line-ups, it was clear to all that hired hands were superior to poor peasants, who were superior to lower-middle peasants, who were superior to middle peasants, who were superior to well-to-do middle peasants ... and so everyone was carefully classified. Before squabbling with a neighbour you had to figure out whether his class status was higher or lower than yours. Only reckless teenagers neglected to do this. But after a few beatings-up they learned not to take on people whose parents had a higher social status.

A boy might sigh, "What foul luck, being the son of a well-to-do middle peasant. People keep jeering that he tried to take the capitalist road and become a rich peasant or landlord."

"Who are you to complain? Look at the kids of landlords and rich peasants. They have to hide their heads like tortoises!"

"Serves them right. Grandchildren pay for their grandparents' crimes."

"Huh, if my dad were a poor or lower-middle peasant, my elder brother'd be able to join the army."

"A lot you know! There are all sorts of poor and

lower-middle peasants. Some of 'em have a bad political record and suspicious contacts. Their ancestry doesn't stand up to investigation. . . ."

As for checking up on the cadres' history, that was even more stimulating. The work team had stipulated that all the cadres must come clean to the Party and the revolutionary masses, to "pass the socialist test". The town's tax-officer had been highly respected because he had fought as a guerrilla. But he admitted to coming from a bureaucrat landlord family and to having seduced one of the family's maids before he joined the guerrillas, after which he had mended his ways. . . . Heavens, so their tax-officer was such a scoundrel! He looked so honest but was an old womanizer! Next time he dunned them for taxes they'd bawl him out.

Then there was the manager of the supply and marketing co-op. He had snivelled and wept at a meeting, saying that though he came from a poor family and his forefathers, all hired hands, had slaved like oxen, once he stood up he had forgotten his roots and soon after Liberation had married a capitalist's daughter. So his family and connections were complicated; but now that they had five children he couldn't get a divorce. . . . Son-in-law of a capitalist, fancy that! How could such a rotter manage the co-op? Next time they had words they would curse him to his face as a capitalist's agent and henchman.

And then there was the accountant of the credit co-op. At one meeting he disclosed that although he'd been born in a slum he had been press-ganged before Liberation and served for three years in the puppet army. So the townsfolk nicknamed him Puppet Soldier Accountant. . . .

There were so many such cases, someone made up a jingle:

> When cadres come clean
> What a bad lot we find them to be.
> Now peasants should control landlords,
> But landlords control you and me!

The Hibiscus market, formerly held at five-day intervals, was now held on Sundays for the convenience of the townsfolk, miners and factory workers in the vicinity. A public security committee was set up to control the market, headed by Wang Qiushe who had joined the Party during the Four Clean-ups Movement and was now Party secretary of Hibiscus Brigade. This committee made a negative example of Hu Yuyin, the new rich peasant who had made so much money by selling beancurd. It kept a strict eye on all capitalist trends. Its members wore yellow armbands and were responsible for curbing speculation and checking up on traders who sold farm or mountain products at high prices. They confiscated those goods which were a state monopoly. So every market day their office was filled with fresh mushrooms, fish, frogs and meat. As these things could not be handed in to the state to increase the public revenue, at first they were left to go bad, which was very wasteful. Later they hit on the method of selling them off cheap as low-quality goods. This had three advantages: it eliminated waste, provided the committee with funds, and after they had rampaged through the market with their yellow armbands each had a share of fresh mountain or water products. In the past, township soldiers had received a small allowance to buy straw sandals. Naturally Chairman Wang

Qiushe remembered this, and he delivered some of these confiscated goods to the commune canteen, to improve Li Guoxiang's diet. Later this public security committee changed its name to the "militia squad", which made it more prestigious and powerful. Any capitalist small fry who surfaced to sell mountain or water products wished they could sink into the ground when they saw this militia squad out to "exercise complete dictatorship over the bourgeoisie". Sometimes, however, these militiamen hid their yellow armbands in their pockets and went about incognito until they had made a haul, when they whisked them out. Haha! No fox, however wily, can escape a keen-eyed hunter. No capitalism, however underhand, can escape our militia! After these "contraband goods" had been confiscated their owners seldom protested, because if they had they would have been arrested and a call would have been put through to their brigade to send militiamen to escort them back.... As time went by some of the more backward hill people secretly called these men "state-subsidized bandits".

Another small revolutionary measure in Hibiscus deserves a mention. Every morning while the revolutionary masses were still in bed, the vicious Rightist Qin Shutian and the new rich peasant's widow Hu Yuyin were penalized by being made to sweep the flagstone street.

But history is implacable, unlike a girl who lets herself be tricked out. Modern Chinese history has often defeated its opponents by surprise tactics and even held up its heroes to ridicule.

After Hibiscus was made a revolutionary model for the whole county, Li Guoxiang was acclaimed as a pace-setter for her "flexible application of politics". Before long, because the revolution needed capable young women path-breakers, she was appointed a member of the county revolutionary committee and Party secretary of this commune. To consolidate the achievements of the Four Clean-ups she still spent most of her time behind the high wall of the Hibiscus Supply and Marketing Co-op.

But in less than half a year, before she had warmed the seat of her office chair, a more tempestuous movement engulfed Hibiscus. For a few days she panicked, then took her stand in the vanguard of this new movement to lead it. First she hauled out the tax-officer and other "revisionists" with the Five Categories and paraded them through the town. Before she had gained full control of the movement, however, some trouble-makers rebelled and put up posters denouncing her. Having discovered that the head of the supply and marketing co-op and the accountant of the credit co-op were behind this, she immediately organized revolutionary cadres like Wang Qiushe and the masses to launch a counter-attack against these Rightists posing as Leftists. It was another mortal combat in which anyone who vacillated or weakened would be trampled underfoot.

But this was the time when Red Guards were roving the country to fan the flames of revolution, and they suddenly descended on Hibiscus like heavenly troops. Defying laws human and divine, and backed by members of the Central Committee, they kicked aside the Party committee to make revolution and turned the small town upside-down. They even challenged Leftists, and actually made a raid on Li Guoxiang's home. Then the fat was in the fire. For on the bed of this unmarried Party secretary they discovered some contraceptives. In a rage they hung a pair of old shoes* round her neck and paraded her through the street!

Paraded together with Li Guoxiang that day were all the Five Categories, wearing black placards. Heaven knows what they thought on finding her in their ranks. They kept their heads lowered, their furtive eyes on the flagstones below their feet. Only the Rightist Qin Shutian turned round to stare at her. Their four eyes, meeting, flashed. Qin's glance was scornful, ironic; Li Guoxiang's was as cold as steel. After two seconds Qin looked away and trudged forward, backing down because the Red Guards had cracked their belts with brass buckles. Li Guoxiang was thoroughly mortified by having not only a black placard round her neck but that pair of old shoes too.

"I assure you, there's some mistake, Red Guards, comrades-in-arms," she insisted. "How can you lump me together with the Five Categories, class enemies? I've never been a Rightist. In 1957, in the County Bureau of Commerce, I was in charge of investigating Rightists. In '59 I joined the county committee to oppose Rightist trends. In '64 and '65 I was the head of the work team to ferret out class enemies and new rich peasants and to struggle against the old Rightists.... Ever since I started working for the revolution I've been a genuine Leftist! So young path-breakers, comrades-in-arms, you shouldn't have nabbed me. New Leftists shouldn't crack down on old Leftists."

The Red Guards hooted with laughter. "Bitch! Who

---

* "Old shoes" in Chinese stands for a loose woman.

are you to talk about Leftists? New Leftists nabbing old Leftists, eh? Vicious slander! A frenzied counter-attack! We're struggling against counter-revolutionary revisionists."

The Red Guards, rough and high-handed, talked with a northern accent and silenced Li Guoxiang by lashing her with their belts.

What was the world coming to? In those fantastic times, truth and falsehood, good and evil, right and wrong had all been mixed up in one simmering witches' cauldron. The innocent had to put up with humiliation and drag out a wretched existence. Bitter factionalism led to wild excesses.

Now a stone bridge was to be built over the river, making Hibiscus accessible to motor-vehicles. The Five Categories had to do unpaid labour carrying stones and sieving sand, for which they received their midday meal on the worksite. Li Guoxiang absolutely refused to sieve sand with the new rich peasant widow Hu Yuyin. Instead she gritted her teeth to go it alone and carry stones up the scaffolding. She never for a moment forgot her status or her superiority to these black devils with whom she had been lumped. The day was bound to come when she would be cleared, when a distinction would be drawn between Leftists and Rightists.

These class enemies' rice ration was three ounces each. The hot sun and heavy work made them pour with sweat, so that these three ounces of rice plus a helping of eggplant with paprika or boiled pumpkins barely took the edge off their hunger. But in the afternoon no one could slack, and so the black-hearted devils asked for more. Only Yuyin found three ounces of rice enough. As Li Guoxiang had previously done very little manual labour, all this hard work increased her appetite and after the meal she still felt ravenous. The Red Guards supervising them devised a way to punish these social outcasts: they could have second helpings if they performed a "devil's dance" from the door of the workshed where they ate to the canteen window some fifteen metres away. The movements of this dance were explained to them.

"Qin Shutian! Before you were made a Rightist you taught music and sport in a middle school and directed a song-and-dance ensemble. Now give your fellow riff-raff a demonstration!"

Qin Shutian at once went to the door of the workshed, showing an alacrity both laughable and disgusting to make an exhibition of himself. After asking once more about the movements of this "devil's dance" and thinking it over briefly, without a glance at anyone he started dancing. His bowl in one hand, his chopsticks in the other, he waved them this way and that, half crouching with his knees apart as he pranced forward, yelling in time with his movements: "Black-hearted devils want more! Black-hearted devils want more. . . ."

The Red Guards clapped and cheered. Commune members who had gathered to watch roared with laughter.

"Encore, Qin Shutian!" they shouted.

"Dance that three times a day, Crazy Qin, and you'll count as reformed — we'll take off your label!"

But the rest of the Five Categories were flabbergasted. Some were as livid as if newly risen from the dead. Some hung their heads and turned away, for fear the Red Guards or revolutionary masses might call on them to do this "devil's dance". But no one panicked or wept. They were like stones in a cess-pool, hard and stinking, used to humiliation of every kind. They had long since forgotten the meaning of "self-respect".

The cook instead of laughing simply gaped. Well, wonders never cease. Reading the little red book, singing and reciting quotations from the Chairman's works every day, overthrowing everything old, smashing Buddhas, razing temples, raiding homes, and now this "devil's dance" ... were these the new culture, new ideology and new customs of the "great cultural revolution"? That cook must have failed to harden his heart and think like a genuine proletarian, for when he filled Qin Shutian's bowl his hands trembled and tears started to his eyes.

That day Li Guoxiang felt famished. As soon as the Red Guards and revolutionary masses had stopped laughing so uproariously she set off with her empty rice bowl to the window. Apparently she wanted to show that she was different from the Five Categories. But the Red Guards insisted on treating her as a monster.

"Halt! Where are you going?"

"You bitch! About face! Parade step to the door!"

One of the Red Guards, a girl, stepped behind her brandishing a broad leather belt. For fear of being beaten Li Guoxiang hastily retreated to the door. Forcing a smile she said, "Little comrades-in-arms! I've had enough, I don't want a second helping."

"Who are you calling your comrades-in-arms? So you've had enough, have you? Why put on such airs? Who are you trying to impress? To challenge? Think you're a cut above the other monsters? Never mind whether you want more or not, you're to do the 'devil's dance' like the Rightist Qin from this door to that window."

"Yes! This 'comrade-in-arms' must dance!"

"Look, with her oval face, snaky waist and long hands and feet, she should be a good dancer."

"If she won't dance, make her crawl there!"

The Red Guards were all shouting at her at once. For some strange reason these young path-breakers who stopped at nothing had a special contempt and hatred for Li Guoxiang.

"Young generals, comrades, honestly I can't dance. I've never danced in my life. Don't be angry, don't whip me, I'll crawl, I'll crawl to the window. . . ."

Tears in her eyes, Li Guoxiang crawled off like a dog.

Leftism carried to an extreme had turned into a boomerang. Leftists who had delighted in crushing others were now under fire themselves. This is what Buddhists call "retribution".

At the end of 1968 when the county revolutionary committee was set up, Li Guoxiang was cleared, declared a revolutionary Leftist and co-opted on to the revolutionary committee and made chairman of the commune. She had no cause for resentment or complaint. As she herself had pointed out in each political movement, at the start when the masses were being mobilized it was hard to avoid slight excesses, the problem was how to control and lead the masses. One couldn't pour cold water to dampen their enthusiasm. Especially in this "great proletarian cultural revolution unprecedented in history", it was only to be expected that for a while Leftists would attack Leftists and good people would gun for each other.

## "Spreading the Gospel"

Fantastic times give rise to fantastic happenings, which were indeed most solemnly enacted throughout the length and breadth of our great land. Readers born since then must regard them as incredible aberrations. But this was one page in our country's unhappy history.

Wang Qiushe, Party secretary of Hibiscus Brigade, went north with a delegation from the county to learn from the experience of other communes — an epoch-making event in this remote little town in the Wuling Mountains. When they left the county to join other delegations in the district, their coach was decorated with red silk and flags, and they were seen off with fire-crackers, gonging and drumming. They had an even more impressive send-off at the district railway station. And they travelled by a special carriage. Not knowing what a special coach or carriage was, the townsfolk who had never left Hibiscus had to ask the Rightist Qin Shutian. He seemed to know all the answers, having read so many books and seen so much of the world, fattening himself on the blood of the labouring people. So it was his duty to enlighten them. He said there were special cars exclusively for leaders, and special coaches to take people to important conferences. Just as in the old days an official's status could be seen from the trappings of his sedan-chair, today different leaders had their different transport. County heads, for instance, had jeeps with canvas roofs,

"Listen to this stinking diehard!" someone protested. "Ask him a question and he grabs at the chance to attack socialism!"

"Well, you asked me," countered Qin with an abject look. "Whatever I say you call it vicious slander. So don't ask me any more questions. If you do, I won't answer them, to keep out of trouble."

"What are special carriages?" someone else insisted.

Qin had to explain that a passenger train had eleven carriages with more than a thousand seats. To ensure the comfort and safety of great men like Vice-commander-in-chief Lin Biao, the only people allowed to accompany him on his special train were his staff, doctors, nurses and guards. He could work, hold meetings, eat and sleep on the train. And other traffic had to make way for it at each station, junction, bridge or tunnel.... Now certain important delegations going to attend a conference also travelled by special trains. So their brigade secretary was getting the same privileged treatment as a provincial head, travelling north by special coach and train.

The Hibiscus townsfolk also heard that when Wang Qiushe, on his return, alighted at the district station where the revolutionary masses had assembled to welcome the delegates with gongs, drums, fire-crackers and flags, he had waved his little red book over his head. They knew he had learned that from a film of Vice-commander-in-chief Lin. And he had kept shouting, "Long live the red sun! Long live the red sun!..." It was said that the county revolutionary committee had sent a jeep to the station. All the way back, a hundred *li* and more, he kept on shouting slogans. After lunching with the county heads he went back by jeep to Hibiscus, still shouting slogans. Only he had caught a chill and his voice was hoarse.

Winter days are short. When darkness fell the stilt-house was brightly lit. Cadres and commune members came to greet Wang, make reports, ask for instructions or simply watch the fun. When one lot left another arrived. One family who hoped the brigade would find their daughter a job brought a big vat of sweet-potato liquor and set it on the square table by the hearth to refresh Secretary Wang after his journey. In his jubilation he forgot his exhaustion and insisted on all the cadres and poor and lower-middle peasants joining him in a drink. As for the middle and well-to-do middle peasants, he simply smiled and nodded at them. So those qualified to drink raised their cups to congratulate him on his triumphant return.

"Secretary Wang! Seems you travelled thousands of *li* by special car and train, and ate special grub for a whole month. All you missed out on was flying!"

"Yes, I didn't fly. But planes aren't too safe. Nowadays the higher-ups prefer special cars and trains. . . ."

"Now that you've been all that way, seen so much of the world and brought back valuable experience, you must tell us all about it!"

"Dazhai is the red banner in agriculture. There's no end to what the whole country must learn from them. Of course I'll tell you about it, so that we can turn our Hibiscus into a model commune."

"Customs change with the times. Tripitaka made his pilgrimage to the West on a white horse, taking only his three disciples Monkey, Pigsy and Sandy. . . . Now our Secretary Wang's had mechanized transport on his pilgrimage north, with tens of thousands of other delegations from all parts of the country. . . ."

"What's that? Are you tipsy, uncle, dragging in Tripitaka? That was feudal superstition, their pilgrimage. *We* want to revolutionize agriculture! If the higher-ups heard you, you'd be in for it."

"In such a big country, Secretary Wang, our Hibiscus only counts as a small fingernail."

"Hibiscus isn't all that small; besides it's very important. The county only sent three heads of brigades on this trip."

These eager questions and tributes made Wang crease his eyes in a smile as he sipped the liquor and munched freshly fried peanuts. Hoarse as he was he answered every question.

"Is it true, Secretary Wang, that over ten thousand people from all parts of the country go there every day?" one youngster asked.

"Yes, from north, south, east and west. Minority people from Yunnan, Xinjiang and Tibet go there too. All the schools, halls and hostels are packed. That hostel we stayed in must be as long as our flagstone street," replied Wang.

"Say, do they use chemical fertilizer?" the youngster asked again.

Wang didn't know what he was driving at. "Of course the state guarantees them a supply, a model place, a red banner for the whole country. But the main thing about them is their self-reliance."

"If ten thousand people go there every day and spend even only one night there, think of all their shit and piss! That brigade's not more than nine hundred *mu*; with all that manure I'd expect the crops to shoot up then flop and not form ears. Why should they need chemical fertilizer too?"

Everybody in the stilt-house roared with laughter.

Before Wang could take this youngster to task for having such stupid notions although his class origin was impeccable, in came Secretary Li Mangeng. During the Four Clean-ups Movement the work team had wanted to expel him from the Party, but as he had admitted his mistake and handed in Hu Yuyin's money, he had been let off lightly and simply demoted.

"You're late, Secretary Li! Wouldn't your wife let you go? I was just going to send for you," drawled Wang, his face red and shining, not troubling to get up. He pointed at a stool and poured Mangeng a cup of liquor.

"Well, what's been happening here while I was up north?"

Li Mangeng was Wang Qiushe's subordinate now, though in the past he had thoroughly despised him. So this reversal of their positions irked him. Still he was no longer the simple-minded ex-soldier he had been ten years ago, but a family man. He gave Wang a brief résumé of recent events in Hibiscus, the daily readings and recitations from Chairman Mao's works in each team, the number of "supreme instructions" written up at each end of the town, and the number of glorious images of the Chairman which had been painted.

"But the townsfolk seem to have some muddled ideas." Wang looked stern. "You haven't stressed politics enough. Just now, dammit if someone didn't compare my fact-finding trip to the north to Tripitaka's pilgrimage to the West. And someone said Dazhai, the red banner of our whole country, shouldn't need any chemical fertilizer because the shit of ten thousand visitors a day would be more than enough to flatten its maize and wheat — isn't that ridiculous? They were poor and lower-middle peasants who said that, but some of the Five Categories must have given them the idea. This is a new trend in class struggle! If we don't crack down on class enemies, they'll attack us!"

Mangeng nodded. So did the others, though some of them were laughing up their sleeves.

"What valuable experience have you brought back, Secretary Wang?" asked Mangeng to change the subject.

"Rich experience. Enough to last us for several lifetimes. Including something we'd never even heard of. If I hadn't seen it with my own eyes I'd never have dreamed of it." Wang took another swig of sweet-potato liquor.

"Go on, tell us about it, Secretary Wang!" Mangeng had a drink too and munched a couple of peanuts.

"It's a whole ceremony called 'three loyalties and four infinites'." Wang rose to his feet, his eyes flashing, fished the little red book out of his pocket and held it to his chest. He seemed as if tranported to some holy land, wearing a halo. "Of all the thousands of things Dazhai has learned, the most important is stressing politics. Every morning they 'ask for instructions'; every evening they 'make a report'. This is done too now on the trains, in bus stations, different organizations and schools."

The novelty of this held everyone's attention.

"When are you going to tell the cadres and masses about this?" Mangeng asked.

"It can't wait!" croaked Wang. "This time we won't

stick to the rule of first notifying Party members and cadres. Go to brigade headquarters, Old Li, and broadcast this announcement: We're holding a mass meeting now in the market-place. Everyone's to bring his little red book. The Five Categories and their families aren't to come."

"You're fagged out after your journey and you've been drinking, why not wait till tomorrow. . . ." Mangeng made no move.

"Secretary Li! Politics takes top priority! This can't wait till tomorrow. Tell everyone to bring the little red book." Glaring, Wang repeated his order.

An hour or so later the old stage in the market-place was brightly lit up by the paraffin lamp. Below were a dark huddle of heads and a sprinkling of glowing pipes and cigarettes. These last few years the townsfolk had grown accustomed to turning out for mass meetings whenever summoned, day or night, to express enthusiastic support for some new editorial or "supreme instruction" and to parade in celebration of it. . . . Wang Qiushe mounted the stage escorted by some brigade cadres, who seated themselves on two benches on this rostrum. Secretary Li Mangeng, standing under the paraffin lamp, called the names of the different team leaders to check the number of people present. When the team farthest away had arrived, he declared the meeting open and announced that Party Secretary Wang would give the revolutionary masses an account of his delegation's trip.

Amid hearty applause Wang stepped to the front of the stage, waving his hand and nodding. Not till the clapping ended did he start gruffly:

"Poor and lower-middle peasants, revolutionary comrades! Have you all brought your little red books?"

People immediately groped in their pockets, many of them shouting:

"Yes, we have!"

"We've brought the selected works!"

"Why doesn't the brigade give us each a pocket edition?"

"Fine, all hold up your little red books!" Wang eyed the market-place as the commune members raised them above their heads. "Good! A sea of red! From now on, going to the fields, knocking off work or attending meetings, you must carry those all the time. Never go anywhere without them, to keep close to the red sun! When you sing, sing quotations. When you read, read the little red book!"

These opening remarks reduced the meeting-place to solemn silence.

"I've just had the honour of going north to gain experience with the delegation from our county and district. We travelled thousands of *li*, spent over a month. Dazhai is a red banner for the whole country, a model in agriculture. People from all over China and abroad are learning from it. Dazhai has whole lots of valuable experience. For instance they award work-points for politics and run political night schools. Their poor and lower-middle peasants are in charge of the schools, of supply and marketing, sanitation, culture and sport. They've done away with private plots and markets. But, above all, they lay stress on politics! Class struggle is what counts, they read the Chairman's works every day and are loyal to our leader. So the gist of their experience is 'three loyalties and four infinites'. Up here in the mountains we didn't know about that. But now I've brought you word of it and I'll show you what it means, so that every morning you can 'ask for instructions' and every evening make your 'report'."

The commune members found this intriguing and mystifying. Wang Qiushe broke off at this point to look at the back wall of the stage. Finding nothing there he asked Mangeng irately, "What's the meaning of this? Why haven't you hung a glorious image on that wall? Go and fetch one at once! There's one in the primary school. Look sharp! You shouldn't have overlooked something so important!"

At once Mangeng jumped down from the stage and dashed to the primary school, while Wang continued to expatiate on the "three loyalties" and "four infinites" and the morning and evening rituals. Soon Mangeng panted back, covered with sweat and dust, a portrait of the Chairman in his hands. As they had no paste or drawing-pins at hand, Wang ordered him to hold the painting up carefully and reverently in the middle of the stage.

"Now, comrades, all hold up your little red books and stand up facing the red sun!" Wang boomed. His audience at once did this.

Wang then gave a demonstration. Standing to attention, chest out and head thrown back, he gazed into the distance, his left arm at his side, his right elbow bent to clasp the little red book to his heart. He then stood sideways looking at the glorious image and recited:

"First we salute our most respected and beloved great leader, great teacher, great commander-in-chief, great helmsman, the red red sun in our hearts — long life to him! May he live for ever! We wish our respected Vice-commander-in-chief Lin good health! May he always enjoy good health!"

Wang had raised his little red books level with his head to wave it rhythmically during this incantation. ... Carried away by his own splendid performance, his throat hoarse, his eyes filled with hot tears, he felt boundless strength and pride. He exulted like a votary who has long cultivated virtue and finally mastered the Way. At that instant, if required to, he would not have hesitated to climb a hill of swords, plunge into a sea of fire, dash his brains out or shed his hot blood. ... Next he made an impassioned speech urging the revolutionary masses and cadres to go straight into action to prove their loyalty. Each production team must hold a ceremony every morning and evening, to turn Hibiscus Commune into a splendid revolutionary school. ... By now Mangeng was worn out, his hands and legs ached from holding up the portrait; but he dared not move — he had to prove his loyalty.

Soon after Wang Qiushe's return with this experience, the commune's revolutionary committee sent in a report to the county. The authorities there with their political acumen realized that this was the newest innovation of the "great proletarian cultural revolution"; to neglect it would be criminal and lead to trouble. At once they declared Wang Qiushe a model for the whole county and invited him to their office to give a demonstration of the morning and evening ritual. They then sent him out by jeep to pass on his experience to all the communes in the county. So Wang Qiushe's name became a household word. But this made him swollen-headed and, since his educational level was low and he lacked political experience, he misjudged the situation and parroted denunciations of capitalist-roaders, including the former county secretary Yang Min'gao and the former commune secretary Li Guoxiang, who had been relieved of their posts. This false move was to cost him dearly. But more of that later.

Here I would like to point out that this spate of modern superstitions was a new variety of the benighted feudal ideas which had prevailed in China for thousands of years — it cannot be ascribed to any single leading figure. Things have to be seen in historical perspective. Have to be studied carefully, dispassionately and objectively, to find the root of the trouble and remedy it. However, there is no need here to probe into when and where this modern cult originated. We can leave the performance of Wang Qiushe of Hibiscus to speak for itself.

## A Tipsy View of the World

Gu Yanshan, the "soldier from the north", was now known as a confirmed drunkard. Because when he had been suspected of having an affair with Hu Yuyin, to whom he had sold state grain, he had been forced to undergo a medical examination in the county hospital. To him that was an unspeakable torture. Though Old Gu had longed for years for a home of his own and a happy family, he had never been willing to pay such a price. But now there was no escaping it. In a spotless white room, where the sunshine streaming in had dazzled his eyes, he was ordered to strip naked.

A crowd of interns in white coats and masks gathered round. They bent over him, prodded and pinched him, then exchanged meaningful glances. Lying motionless like a castrated stallion, all over goose-flesh and dripping with cold sweat, he shivered and closed his eyes, his mind a blank. . . . He had been wounded in the thigh near Tianjin by KMT troops. Blood had soaked through his padded trousers and he had thought he was going to die, to leave this land so soon to be liberated. His mind was a blank then too. But comrades-in-arms had rescued him, and after an old peasant woman had nursed him for over a month he went back to his unit. Of course he wasn't going to die this time either. . . . Who had gunned for him this time? And what sort of battle was this? It was to combat revisionism and capitalism, to root out bourgeois ideas and promote what was proletarian, to ensure that China would remain socialist and prevent another blood-bath. So everyone must pass the test and undergo a thorough examination, both mental and physical. This involved much more than taking up arms to fight the enemy. It was much more complex and bewildering. . . . After what seemed an endless examination a male nurse told him to go out and put on his clothes. Through the door, left ajar, he heard the doctors' diagnosis: "The fellow is impotent." Someone — probably an ingenuous intern — asked softly, "Is he a hermaphrodite? Someone who switches sexes?" The doctors' hoots of laughter, as if this were a prize joke, shook the window-panes. Old Gu wished that Old Man Heaven would send an earthquake to swallow him up along with that mocking laughter.

The work team reported to the county committee that

as Gu Yanshan had lost his class stand completely and exerted such a bad influence, for years fostering capitalist forces, he should be expelled from the Party and sent home to labour. But some veterans in the county committee recalled that he was a cadre from the north who had previously committed no mistakes; so although his attitude had been bad and he had not made a serious self-criticism, he should be allowed a way out. They decided to let him off with a stern reprimand and reduce his salary, then watch his subsequent behaviour.

Before long the higher-ups assigned a new number-one man to Hibiscus Grain Depot. Although Old Gu was not removed from his post, he did not "come downstairs". Well, he was used to living upstairs, and he had not committed suicide.

With no official duties he took life easy. The next year the storm of the "cultural revolution" swept down on them. But Old Gu took no part in it, drinking to drown his sorrows. Often he drank himself tipsy, then told the children stories of doughty drinkers, heroes of old like Wu Song, who killed a tiger in his cups. He knew no end of such legends and the children never tired of listening to them, never denounced him either for "peddling black feudal, bourgeois and revisionist wares".

That winter, Old Gu heard that Mangeng's wife Peppery had brewed a vat of maize liquor, real fire-water, and had raised a black dog which now weighed a dozen catties. So one evening he went to their home through the whirling snow, taking sixty yuan to buy the liquor and dog, meaning to have a good binge with Mangeng. As Mangeng had been down on his luck for the last few years, under the thumb of Wang Qiushe he had to do what he was told, but sometimes was given a rap on his knuckles. They put the black dog in a sack and drowned it in the river, then took it home and scoured off its fur with lime, turning it into a plump white hairless dog. Next they lit the fire, cut up the dog and fried it with tea-seed oil, then simmered it with spices.

Eating dogflesh in snowy weather has always been one of the favourite treats of grown-ups and children alike in the Wuling Mountains. And as it so happened, this evening Peppery had taken her daughters home to her mother, there was no one to stop these two fellows from boozing.

Mangeng boasted, "I'm going to drink you under the table."

Old Gu said, "We must smash this vat of yours this evening."

At first they drank from wine cups, then switched to mugs and finally to rice bowls.

"Drink up, dammit! I've never been really pissed, so I don't know what my capacity is." Old Gu clinked bowls with Mangeng, then tossed off his liquor.

"That's the style, drink up! Years ago I made one wrong move, and since then everything has gone wrong ... all because of a woman — damn all women. Drink up! I'm treating you to this liquor." After draining his bowl Mangeng slapped it down on the table.

"A woman? There are all sorts of women, some the salt of the earth, some real devils.... Can't lump them all together. Here, give me another drink." Old Gu held out his empty bowl.

They were still only half tipsy. For fear of making a

gaffe Mangeng kept quiet. Old Gu found his boastfulness ridiculous. He had pocketed the sixty yuan yet said he was standing treat. Son of a tortoise, it's Old Gu who's treating you!

Toasting and trying to outdrink each other they emptied bowl after bowl. By degrees they felt buoyant yet brimming with strength, high spirits and confidence, as if able to trample the world underfoot. They now picked up their chopsticks and stuffed fat dogflesh into each other's mouths.

"Brother Gu! Old soldier, eat this chunk for me, dammit, even if it were a chunk of human flesh."

"Mangeng, there are people nowadays with hearts like iron, fiercer than tigers. Real cannibals they are! Yet they're the ones favoured by the higher-ups.... To be heartless, is that revolution? The way to struggle?"

"A revolutionary won't recognize kith and kin! You must harden your heart to struggle...."

"You've said it, ha! Drink up!"

The more they drank, the more they warmed to each other, and the more worked up they grew.

"Mangeng! You say, is that woman Li Guoxiang any good? The piddling manager of a restaurant, she suddenly changed into the head of a work team. Things had been fine in our Hibiscus till she turned it topsy-turvy, with no peace for man or beast! Then she suddenly changed into one of the county committee, our commune secretary.... How did she shoot up like that?... Till those Red Guards who stop at nothing hung old shoes round her neck and paraded her through the street...."

The liquor had gone to Old Gu's head. In a rage

he staggered to his feet, cursing and pounding the table. Cups, bowls, dishes and chopsticks clattered.

Mangeng spat out a dog bone and bellowed with laughter.

"That woman can't dance the 'devil's dance' but she can crawl like a dog.... What a joke! She's not bad-looking, but a holy terror, the things she says and does.... When I worked in the district government, her uncle — he was district secretary — tried to foist this hell-cat on me.... I was a fool ... if I'd agreed, she'd be under my thumb today! At very least I'd be top man in the commune."

"Don't lose heart. Not many hell-cats, even in history, have crawled over men's heads to shit on them. Crazy Qin in your brigade told me there was Lü Zhi of Han, Wu Zetian of Tang, the Empress Dowager of Qing.... The truth is, brother, that Rightist Qin isn't such a bad lot as most of the Five Categories...."

"Don't give me that talk, Old Gu, an old revolutionary like you from the north. Haven't you been denounced right and left, haven't I had to make endless self-criticisms, all because of Crazy Qin! All those recantations I wrote — too superficial. The work team all but made me kneel on shards. To hell with it.... I'm through with caring about other people. I can harden my heart and get tough, what do I care if the Five Categories change into pigs or dogs, if they live or die.... What matters is getting by myself with Peppery and the girls...."

"You should have a heart, Mangeng. Can't you see that the one worst up against it in Hibiscus is that young widow? Has Peppery stuffed your eyes up the crotch of her pants?"

Drink both clears the mind and befuddles it. Old Gu's eyes were red, either from drinking or from weeping.

At this mention of Yuyin, Mangeng's eyes glazed over.... After a while he said, "My sister! No, she's a rich peasant now. I made a clean break with her long ago ... poor woman.... What a fool I am! A fool!" He suddenly burst out laughing, then abruptly wiped the smile off his face, his expression wooden again. "A fool, that's what I am.... I was too young, took things too seriously.... Didn't marry her, the Party wouldn't let me, but ... if...."

"If what? Don't talk with your mouth full of dog bones!" Old Gu stared at him aggressively.

"Fact is, the truth is, brother, when I think of her my heart aches...."

"Still sweet on her? Seems to me you wronged her, hit her when she was down.... It was cruel what you did to save your own hide! She looked on you as her brother, gave you one thousand five hundred to keep for her, and you handed it in to the work team as her loot from profiteering, a proof of her capitalist crimes.... Brother and sister are like birds in the same wood, who fly off in different directions in time of danger!"

"Old Gu! Old Gu!... Don't!" Mangeng beat his chest, tears streaming down his cheeks. "Each word you say cuts like a knife....I couldn't help myself, couldn't! Fighting the enemy I gritted my teeth, ready to die rather than desert.... But up against the Party, the work team from the county, what could I do? You tell me! I was afraid of being expelled from the Party! Hell, I can't lose my Party membership. ..."

"Aha, Li Mangeng! This evening I spent sixty yuan to buy this vat of liquor and dog — and this admission of yours!" Old Gu bucked up on hearing the former Party secretary of the commune sob uncontrollably. He laughed and bellowed, "So your heart's not completely black and hard. Not everyone in Hibiscus has a heart of stone!"

". . . Brother, you're still the 'soldier from the north' looked up to by the whole town. A rough diamond. . . ."

"So you still have some human feeling, brother!" Old Gu crowed. "You still have some feeling!"

They kept this up, laughing and crying till dawn.

When the vat was finally empty, chucking aside their bowls they flopped down, shaking with laughter.

"I'll spare your damned vat to come and drink tomorrow!"

"You're stinking drunk, pissed! Take that dog leg for when you drink in your room upstairs tomorrow!"

"Keep the rest of the dog, Mangeng. . . . I must get back to the grain depot. Haven't 'come downstairs' yet . . . have to stay upstairs. . . ."

The snow was falling softly, as if to cover and conceal all the garbage everywhere. A dim flashlight shone on a trial of uneven footprint to the flagstone street. Luckily the highway bridge had been completed, so there was no need to call up the ferryman.

Old Gu staggered back through the north wind. The liquor had gone to his head, making it reel. Standing in the middle of the street he swore:

"Listen, you! Hell-cat! Slut! What have you done to our town? Even made a clean sweep of our poultry and dogs. Grown-ups and kids, no one dares say a

word. You bitch! You hell-cat! You slut! If you've any
guts, come and have it out with me!..."

His shouts woke the people living on both sides of
the street, and they knew whom the "soldier from the
north" was cursing. As it was freezing, no one got up
to watch or to stop him. Only the staff of the supply
and marketing co-op felt sorry that Li Guoxiang was
not there to hear his curses — she had gone to the county to attend a meeting.

Gu Yanshan was beside himself. That dawn in the
flurrying snow he rampaged up and down the street,
shouting curses. Finally, intoxicated and tired out, he
flopped down at the gate of the co-op. There he vomited
on to the snow. A stray dog running over avidly lapped
up his vomit.... Snoring, Old Gu shook his fist.

"...Keep quiet, Secretary Wang, Chairman Li!
Just smack your lips over your own grub and grog. I'm
drunk, I'm going to sleep.... Smack your lips over
your own grub and grog...."

Old Gu did not freeze to death. For a wonder he
didn't even catch a chill. Before it was light, while
the shops on both sides of the flagstone street were
still closed, he was carried up to his room above the
grain depot. Who carried him? There is no knowing.


## Phoenixes and Hens

Wang Qiushe's tour of the county to demonstrate the
new morning and evening rituals met with loud accla-
mations. Everywhere he was received and sent off with
fire-crackers, drumming and gonging. This style of life
went to his head, for he was treated to more chicken,

duck, fish and meat than he had ever seen before in his life. And while spreading the truth he took an active part in the criticism campaign, denouncing the counter-revolutionary revisionist crimes of Yang Min'gao, the top man in the county, and their commune Party secretary Li Guoxiang. The latter had had to step down to be educated and criticized by the revolutionary masses. She ground her teeth with fury at the way the stilt-house's owner had turned against her, and could have kicked herself for boosting up such a wretch. "Confound it! Talk of lifting a rock and dropping it on your own feet!" she swore at herself. "You made him an activist, sponsored him to join the Party, appointed him secretary of the brigade, and wanted to groom him to be a government cadre. You even took a fancy to this bachelor a little older than you. . . . But now the dog has bitten the hand that fed him! He's forgotten all you did for him and once across the river has torn down the bridge. He's a real snake in the grass, denouncing uncle and me right and left. . . ."

In those days the cadres who had stepped down to be investigated used to recite this jingle:

> When phoenixes are out of luck, hens soar;
> A moulting phoenix isn't up to a hen.
> But when its plumage grows once more
> A phoenix is a phoenix, a hen a hen again.

Li Guoxiang recited this too and took courage from it. And indeed in less than a year it came true for her. When the county revolutionary committee was re-established with Yang Min'gao as its first deputy chairman, she was co-opted as a standing member, concurrently chairman of the revolutionary committee of the commune. Her lovely phoenix plumage had grown again, and she was once more the queen of all feathered creatures.

Poor Wang Qiushe! He had not yet washed the mud from his feet or climbed up to become a state functionary, entitled to ride in a jeep as a full-time propagandist. After he had shone for a year or two, attracting others to follow his example, the rituals he had introduced spread to all corners of the county and new activists emerged who could recite their vows in standard Chinese, unmixed with the local accent, flourish little red books more stylishly and perform a "loyalty" dance. So although he had been a path-breaker, his performance paled by comparison, his historic mission accomplished. In the eyes of the revolutionary masses and cadres, he was no longer a treasure. Before long the higher-ups called upon the mass representatives in different leading bodies to go back to their own units to grasp revolution and promote production. So back he went to Hibiscus as chairman of the brigade. This made him Li Guoxiang's subordinate once more. The phoenix was still a phoenix, the hen a hen.

Remorse is bitter. A year before, Li Guoxiang had regretted boosting up the stilt-house's owner; now he bitterly repented having denounced her in public. But who could be held to blame? Big movements have their stormy ups and downs, and leaders and masses alike have to keep in step with the political situation. . . . Sometimes Wang Qiushe felt tempted to bite off his tongue! He often slapped his mouth, fuming, "Idiot! Dolt! Throwing your weight about! Who made you an activist, sponsored you to join the Party and sent you to Dazhai? Dogs should wag their tails, but you bit the mistress who'd fed you. . . ." After racking his brains it dawned on him that his only hope of getting ahead politically and rising in the world was by sucking up to Li Guoxiang and relying on Yang Min'gao. They were above him in the power structure. He was no numskull. Though remorse was bitter it paid better than being pigheaded.

To revert to Chairman Li Guoxiang, she had quiet quarters on the floor above the Hibiscus Supply and Marketing Co-op. Her outer room, an office and reception room, contained a desk, a wicker armchair and some stools. A portrait of Chairman Mao hung on the wall, which also had pasted on it quotations of his in gold characters on red paper. There was a bookcase for the Chairman's works, as well as a telephone. The predominant colour, red, proclaimed her status and character. We need not describe the inner room, her bedroom, as we are not ingenuous Red Guards who insist on prying into the private life of a spinster in her thirties. After six in the evening, when the co-op closed and its staff went home to their quarters in the back yard, this room was uncannily quiet.

Wang Qiushe had come here several times to make his reports and ask for her instructions. He always halted nervously at the door to smooth his hair and clear his throat; but as Li Guoxiang did not want to see him in private, he had never been admitted. Instead of losing heart he believed his sincerity would eventually move her and enable him to storm this fortress.

"Chairman Li, Party Secretary Li. . . ." Today he knocked softly at her door again.

"Who's there?" She was laughing with somebody inside.

"It's me.... Wang Qiushe...." he stammered, his throat dry.

"What do you want?" Her voice had turned cold and stern.

"I've a little business...."

"We can discuss it later. I'm busy now, studying material."

Wang Qiushe slunk back to the stilt-house, his appetite spoiled. Still, since he was "No. 1" in the brigade, cadres kept coming to consult him or commune members to bring him information. So what with all the new "supreme instructions" and "important documents" sent down from above, he was far from being lonely. One afternoon some days later he spruced himself up. First he went to the barber's shop for a haircut and shave. He had on a smart jacket over his white shirt, newly washed trousers and his pigskin shoes. Not until the townsfolk were at supper and lights had appeared in their windows did he go to the supply and marketing co-op, determined not to leave till he had seen Li Guoxiang and unburdened himself to her.

For some strange reason when he stepped through the side gate of the co-op compound, his heart went pit-a-pat as if he were doing something underhand. Luckily he didn't run into anyone. He stood for a while in front of Li Guoxiang's door before raising his hand to knock.

"Chairman Li, Party Secretary Li...."

"Who is it? Come on in." Her voice was kindly.

Wang Qiushe went in. Li Guoxiang, seated at the round table, was eating a braised chicken.

"So it's you. What do you want? You've come several times, haven't you? Well, tell me your business. I had visitors all afternoon. You'd think they'd come from some drought area the way they emptied my three thermos flasks!"

After a cursory glance at him, Li Guoxiang turned her attention to the braised chicken. But that one glance struck Wang as condescending and ironical — she was treating him like an inferior.

"Chairman Li, I, I want to admit my mistakes to the leadership," he stammered.

"What mistakes? You're a pace-setter here. You've lectured all over the county, you have a good record." She glanced at him again with a show of surprise, and added sarcastically, "Don't be so polite, Secretary Wang. Doesn't the proverb say: A dragon is no match for a local snake. I may be in charge of the commune, but I can't cope with you cadres. Any time you like you can have me dismissed from office!"

"Chairman Li, Party Secretary Li.... Even if you don't jeer or swear at me, I've lost face.... How can I look *you* in the face? ... I'm a good-for-nothing. As soon as I started riding high, I forgot your goodness to me...." His head sagged like a ripe ear of paddy. Shoulders bent he perched himself on a stool and sat there respectfully, his hands on his joined knees.

"Well, what brought you here? Why eat humble pie like this?" she asked as she turned to pick up a chicken leg. In her position she was used to people grovelling to her.

"I'm ... er, too stupid to size up the situation.... I just shouted slogans with everyone else, like a parrot — a real fool I was...." Wang watched her expression, wanting to see her reaction.

"Just say what's on your mind. I never blame anyone

for speaking out; it's hedging I can't abide." She shot him another glance and discovered that this evening he looked quite presentable.

"I want to come clean with you, chairman. I've behaved like a swine, forgetting your goodness to me! I let you down, and County Secretary Yang as well.... You two were the ones who boosted me so that I could join the Party, be a Party secretary.... But I, I parroted the rest of them and, to keep in step, showered filthy abuse on you both.... I could kick myself for that now.... Only wish I could tie myself up for you leaders to punish...." This speech poured out like muddy water from a breach in a pond while his tears plopped on the floor. "You went to such pains to train me, but I let the higher-ups down. Came a great cropper.... Now I want to apologize to you and Secretary Yang and ask for punishment.... I should slap my mouth a thousand times before you...."

At first Li Guoxiang frowned, then looked grave. His remorseful tears seemed to have softened her heart. Looking rather upset, she wiped her greasy hands with her handkerchief and sat back limply in the wicker chair. She felt rather at a loss — but only for a few seconds. Then she straightened up, raised her eyebrows and glanced at him disdainfully again.

"That's ancient history now. Let bygones be bygones. You have a good memory, I've forgotten all that ... and I don't care about it. A bit of abuse and criticism were good for me. I don't want you to harp on it or to make a self-criticism.... And I'm not interested in your remorse...."

"Honestly, Chairman Li, I mean it.... I know how kind and how forgiving you are...." Because she was still giving herself official airs and keeping him at a distance, his heart pounded, his palms sweated, and he felt bitterly frustrated. But there was no backing down now. He must arouse her interest to show her that he was still useful ... he was quite clear-headed now. He recalled the talk he had heard recently about Li Mangeng, secretary of their brigade, and Gu Yanshan who had been toppled during the Four Clean-ups Movement. They had gorged themselves on dog's meat late one night, got stinking drunk and talked a lot of reactionary nonsense. Then the "soldier from the north" had rampaged up and down the street swearing.... Yes, first he'd offer her this "information". In times like these, if you didn't inform on others they'd inform on you.

"Chairman Li, I'd like to take this chance to tell you about some new trends in Hibiscus...."

"What new trends?"

Sure enough, she had turned to face him, her eyes flashing.

"Qin Shutian and the rest of the Five Categories are getting out of hand." Wang deliberately approached his subject indirectly. "The brigade has ordered them to admit their crimes every morning and express repentance every evening, but they actually turn up later than the poor and lower-middle peasants! Nowadays eighty per cent of the brigade join in loyalty exercises and dance the loyalty dance. The only ones too pig-headed to do this are a few of the old folk. They prefer bowing to the glorious image...."

"Don't talk nonsense. The Five Categories are dead tigers. It's the live tigers and snakes that the problem." She fixed him with narrowed eyes. The icy glint in them made Wang Qiushe tremble. But then she decided to bait him. "A revolutionary cadre can't just pay attention to people already labelled: it's more important to keep an eye on those who pass themselves off as the rank and file. . . . What about the old cadres, Gu Yanshan and that lot. Have they been up to anything recently?"

Wang's heart missed a beat. If she already knew about Gu Yanshan and Li Mangeng's escapade, this information of his wouldn't be worth a fart. Still, gritting his teeth, he gave an embroidered account of what had happened, then stated that Li Mangeng wasn't fit to be secretary of the brigade.

"Secretary Wang! Come and sit here and have a drink." To Wang's surprise, this report of his had made Li Guoxiang much more cordial. Turning round she took a bottle and two glasses from the cupboard, as well as a dish of fried peanuts. "Don't think you men are the only ones who can drink. I'll take you on. We'll see who turns red first!"

Wang was overwhelmed by this unexpected favour. He took the bottle, filled both glasses to the brim, then sat down at the table and looked respectfully, unblinkingly, at his hostess.

"Come on. Let's drain this glass!" Li Guoxiang raised her glass and glanced at him from under it. Wang followed suit. Then they clinked glasses and tossed back the wine.

"Here's a chicken leg for you. You have good teeth, polish it off!" To show her trust and friendliness, Li Guoxiang passed him her half-eaten chicken leg. He accepted it with a bow.

"What else has been happening in the brigade, in

town?" she asked, enjoying the gusto with which he was eating.

"There's an ill wind blowing through Hibiscus. The last few years, all sorts of strange fish have surfaced. . . . You may not know, chairman, but the tax-officer who was thrown out and sent home a few years back is now attacking us, asking the provincial and district authorities to clear his case." Wang had lowered his voice and kept glancing at the door.

"So that's one." Li Guoxiang looked grave. "The tax-officer from a bureaucrat landlord family, dismissed during the Four Clean-ups, is trying to reverse his case."

"A new rebel corps has been set up . . . the chairman of the supply and marketing co-op is said to be its secret head. . . . And they want Gu Yanshan to be their adviser, but he's not interested — the drunken sot."

"That's two. A new development, a rebel corps master-minded by the chairman of the co-op, but Gu Yanshan's too befuddled to join in."

Li Guoxiang was making notes now in the notebook which she always carried with her.

"The young assistant in the rice mill. . . ."

"Well?"

"Has had it off with the wife of the credit co-op's accountant."

"Pah! Stop farting! Why report that?"

Li Guoxiang sat back blushing, her hair a little tousled.

"No, that woman let on to the rice mill assistant that her old man is going to the county to denounce you. . . ."

"Ha, that's three. A new development." She kept cool. "You see, if a leading cadre doesn't have a mass line and people to keep tabs on things, it's hard to cope.... Tell me all the other new trends you know about, so that the leadership can take appropriate action."

"That's all for now." Wang was no longer stammering nervously but eating and drinking heartily. He felt he had made good again in her eyes.

"Wang Qiushe!" she snapped sternly.

"Chairman Li...." His legs trembled as he stood up, cringing.

"Sit down, sit down, you're all right...." She rose and paced up and down as if thinking over some important decision. "I'll sort them out one by one. How many guns has your brigade militia?"

"We've one platoon."

"Are you in charge of it?"

"Of course. As brigade secretary." He slapped his chest.

"Good. Don't let bad characters get control of it. No one's to make a move till I give the word."

"I promise to be responsible to you and you only, chairman. I'll do whatever you say."

"Sit down, sit down. There's no need to be so tense." She put her hands on his shoulders and he sat down submissively, rather excited by the warmth and softness of her fingers. "With the power in our hands we needn't use force. It's only those without power who do that. Understand? Taking up arms is a last resort.... As for Li Mangeng we'll have to win him over and keep him under your thumb. One key task of the revolution today is preventing men like Gu Yanshan from staging a come-back, to regain power in Hibiscus, go in for class conciliation, put production first and preach humanistic nonsense.... Understand?"

Wang nodded like a woodpecker, lost in admiration of her wisdom and courage.

Li Guoxiang went back to her wicker chair by the round table. Her hands on its arms, as if tipsy, she stared unblinkingly at the stilt-house owner. "I can tell you frankly, Secretary Wang, I'm delighted that you've turned over a new leaf. We can let bygones be bygones. I need some able assistants and mean to test you.... I'm not promising anything, but if you come up to scratch I'll raise your case some time with Chairman Yang, and see if you can't be relieved of your other duties and made a deputy chairman of the commune...."

What a bolt of spring thunder! Wang's heart palpitated. This was an opportunity not to be missed — it affected his whole future. He sprang to his feet, then dropped down on his knees before her.

"Chairman Li! I, from now on I'm your man... even if people call me a cur... I'll be loyal to you...."

Li Guoxiang started, then smiled complacently and said rather archly, "Get up, get up! Revolting. A cadre shouldn't be so spineless. What if someone saw you...."

Instead of standing up, Wang gazed up at her, his face streaked with tears. Her heart softened, she leaned forward to stroke his hair.

"Get up for goodness' sake. A grown man... just had a haircut? You smell of scented soap. How hot your cheeks are.... I must rest now. I've had too much to drink. These are still early days, go on home...."

Wang stood up, wide-eyed with infatuation, and gazed at her as if longing for some sign or order.

## Among Monsters

Qin Shutian and Hu Yuyin of the Five Categories had been penalized for two or three years by having to sweep the flagstone street every morning. Both got up very early. They usually started sweeping from the middle of the street to both ends, taking half each. Sometimes they started from the ends and met in the middle. Luckily the street was not wide and little more than three hundred metres long. So every day of the year, while the townsfolk were still dreaming blissfully, they took their bamboo brooms and swept in silence. Their brooms seemed to sweep away, then sweep back again spring, summer, autumn and winter.

Qin Shutian swept with style, having once been the director of a song-and-dance ensemble. Holding himself erect, with his right hand above and his left hand below, he swept with easy strokes like an oarsman on the stage; and his steps were rhythmical. With his nimbleness and good co-ordination he worked fast and well, seldom sweating. And he swept a stretch for Yuyin too every day. The work always made her perspire, and she envied Qin his skill. A woman should have excelled a man at this job.

Crazy Qin's behaviour these years had been contemptible and laughable. During the Four Clean-ups he was the man most fiercely attacked in Hibiscus. Later, the Party secretary of the brigade got the work team's permission to let him go on heading the Five

Categories — "counteracting poison with poison". He was labelled Iron-hat Rightist, to show that this label would go to his grave with him. Fortunately he had no wife and therefore no children to inherit this political legacy. And he knew that revolution needs a target. Unless each village and town kept a few "dead tigers", how could mass movements and struggles be mobilized? Each time the higher-ups urged them to grasp class struggle, the local cadres called meetings, paraded and denounced the Five Categories, then reported the number of class enemies struggled against and recalled their past bitterness to educate the masses. In teams where the Five Categories had died out, their children took their place. Otherwise, how to convince people that in the historical period of socialism there would always be classes, class contradictions and struggles?

As the cadres in the countryside earned workpoints not salaries, they could hardly be called "capitalist-roaders" or "agents of the bourgeoisie". After Land Reform there had been a number of movements to re-define class status. As the means of production had been collectivized, putting an end to private property, the criterion for this was each one's political record. But children could still inherit their parents' class status. . . . Anyway, let us get back now to Crazy Qin.

In 1967, when class struggle was at its height, all the Five Categories had been ordered to place clay effigies of themselves at their gates, to distinguish them from the revolutionary masses who exercised dictatorship over them. Hibiscus Brigade had twenty-two such people, who needed twenty-two clay effigies. This unpaid labour was naturally assigned to Crazy Qin because he could write and draw. He dug up loads of clay and dumped one at the gate of all the Five Categories. This was a job for a craftsman. Spectators gathered every day to make comments. And because he worked overtime, in less than a month he had finished twenty-two men and women, tall, short, lean or fat. On each pedestal he wrote the name and title of the monster whose likeness he had caught. This was one of the wonders of the brigade. Grown-ups and children flocked to look and pass judgement, all agreeing that the effigy at Crazy Qin's gate was most lifelike.

"You selfish swine, Crazy Qin! You only put yourself out over your own statue."

"That wasn't selfishness. Doesn't the Chairman say that life is the only source of literature and art? ... Of course I know myself best, that's why mine's more lifelike."

But Crazy Qin had been seriously deficient, neglecting to make a clay figure of Yuyin, the new rich peasant's widow, for the doorway of the old inn. This "plot" was discovered much later, and at once he was struggled against to find out why he had protected her and what the two of them were really up to. He promptly hung his head and admitted his guilt: he had only remembered the earlier number of Five Categories and forgotten those designated as rich peasants in the Four Clean-ups. He promised to make amends, yet procrastinated till new instructions came down: The struggle against the Five Categories must not remain formalistic; their wrong thinking must be thoroughly exposed so that they really stank. And so no clay figure appeared outside the inn, and for this Yuyin was most grateful to Qin Shutian. The evening that he was denounced she hid in her room, her eyes swollen with weeping. She felt he had saved her life. Because if she had seen children pee on her effigy she would surely have been driven to suicide.

But although formalism was frowned upon, each time the Five Categories were paraded they still had to wear black placards and tall hats. Hibiscus was a small out-of-the-way town near the border of the province. They heard that in Beijing even leading cadres and veteran revolutionaries had black placards hung round their necks in mass struggle meetings. How could Hibiscus compare with the capital? It wasn't even marked on the map of China. It goes without saying that all the black placards worn by their Five Categories were the handiwork of Crazy Qin. To show his public spirit, he made his own extra large. Each placard bore the wearer's "title" followed by a name marked with red crosses, to show that each of them deserved to be shot. And here again he played a trick, not putting any red crosses on the placard of the "new rich peasant Hu Yuyin". Luckily this "plot" of his escaped the vigilant eyes of the masses. Because of this Yuyin, whose bean-curd stall had made her a new rich peasant, had tears of gratitude in her eyes each time she was paraded. It made her feel that in this callous world there still lingered the faint warmth of spring.

The townsfolk said that Crazy Qin had grown glib and slippery after being struggled against in so many movements. Each time the militia called him to a struggle meeting, he went off as calmly as if going off to work. When he was paraded he knew the way and always took his place at the head of the Five Categories' column.

"Qin Shutian!"

"Here!"

"Iron-hat Rightist!"

"Present!"

Sternly challenged, he called back clearly and succinctly.

At the start of the movement to purify the class ranks, a mass mobilization meeting was called by the commune, at which the Five Categories of different brigades were paraded. They were then ordered to wait at the four corners of the meeting-ground while the new policy was explained. But after the meeting dispersed, the militia forgot about them and left them there — a grave lapse in the grave class struggle. It had been announced that they were not to move without the Party secretary's permission, or they would be punished for sabotaging the rally. What was to be done? Would they just have to stay put there? It was Crazy Qin who hit on a solution. He mustered the others and shouted: "Attention! Eyes right! Eyes front! Number off, at ease!" He then stepped forward and clicked his heels, standing to attention to salute the deserted meeting-ground.

"Report, Secretary Li! Secretary Wang!" he announced. "The twenty-three Five Categories of Hibiscus have been criticized and educated at the rally. Please let them go back to their different teams to repent their crimes and reform themselves through labour."

A slight pause followed, during which he pretended to have heard certain instructions.

"Right!" he cried. "We shall carry out the higher-ups' orders and abide by the law. Dismiss!" Having gone through this procedure he sent the others away.

First thing in the morning Hibiscus was wrapped in mist. No dogs or cocks could be heard in the flagstone street. The townsfolk and their livestock were sound asleep as Qin Shutian went with his broom to call up Yuyin. They were the first to see each other every morning. Standing at the gate of the inn they would exchange glances and smiles.

"What an early riser you are, brother. Calling for me every day. . . ."

"I'm ten years older than you, Yuyin. I don't need so much sleep."

"Do you have insomnia?"

"Me? Well yes, it started when I was a teacher."

"What do you do when you can't sleep?"

"I sing songs from *Wedding Songs*."

At mention of this they fell silent. Those songs had involved them both in so much trouble. Little by little these morning encounters of theirs became an indispensable part of their lives. If one of them failed to turn up, the other would feel as upset as if something important were missing. He or she would finish sweeping the street in silence, then go to see what was wrong. Their minds would only be at rest when they met again the next morning to exchange glances and smiles.

One misty morning they began sweeping from the middle of the street, their backs to each other. The only sound in the stillness was the swish of their brooms on the flagstones. At the corner of the supply and marketing co-op, Qin leaned against the wall for a short rest. Suddenly he heard the side gate in the alley creak. He peered round and saw a burly black figure shoot out then shut the gate behind him. "A thief!" His heart missed a beat. But no, the man's hands were empty, he was not encumbered with loot. Consumed with curiosity, Qin watched the fellow make off. He knew that all the staff of the co-op lived in the backyard, only Li Guoxiang lived upstairs. And he thought he recognized the man who had left. What did this mean? He dared not make a sound. That noon he went back to the co-op to have a look, but heard no talk of anything being stolen.

A few days later it dawned clear and fine. Qin and Yuyin parted in the middle of the street to sweep to the ends. At the corner of the co-op wall he stopped to rest again, and this time he peered round before the side gate creaked. When it did a burly black figure shot out again, pulled the gate to behind him and hurried off down the alley. This time Qin had seen him clearly. He was astounded. Heavens, what did he do in that compound every night? The implications of this were so serious, he dared not make it public. But he ran to the other end of the street and called Yuyin into a corner, where he whispered this secret to her.

"Don't breathe a word about this to anyone else," he urged her. "There's nothing the townsfolk can do about it, so we'll have to turn a blind eye. In our position especially...."

"Was it him?"

"Yes."

"With whom?"

"With her."

"Him, her — who the devil knows who you mean." But Yuyin was flushed and smiling. "Hell! Whispering into my ear, you're pricking me with that bristly moustache of yours!"

"All right, all right, I'll shave it off. Shave every day."

Cheek to cheek, looking into each other's eyes, it was the first time they had been so close.

Another morning Qin decided to play a trick. He told Yuyin about it when they met in the middle of the street, and she replied with a smile, "Whatever you say." Breaking their rule for the first time, instead of sweeping the street they shovelled up some cow-dung from the team's ox shed and spread it in front of the co-op's side gate where anyone coming out was bound to tread. Then they hid round the corner, peeking out. Too bad that it was misty again. Unconsciously they nestled close together. After some time they heard footsteps coming downstairs. Qin bent down while Yuyin rested her cheek on his shoulder, both looking in the same direction, so excited and tense they felt they could hear their hearts pounding. When Yuyin leaned round the corner, Qin straightened up and pulled her back, keeping his arm around her and holding her close, the rascal! She had to slap him twice to make him let go.

The side gate creaked, the black shadow flashed out and must have slipped on the cow-dung. They heard a thud like a log falling on to the flagstones. The fellow's head must have taken a hard crack. He lay there groaning, unable to get up.

"Serves him right, the swine!" Yuyin clapped her hands like a child and started giggling.

Qin hastily covered her mouth and glanced at her warningly. The warmth of his hand seemed to find its way to her heart.

The two street-sweepers stood there watching the groaning figure as he tried in vain to get up. It looked as if he had broken a bone. Qin was frightened. Then it occurred to him that here was a chance to "atone for his crimes". He whispered some instructions to Yuyin. But this time his cheeks were smooth shaven and he had no moustache to prick her face. She pushed his hands away and went off to sweep the street.

Qin walked softly back to the middle of the street and set about sweeping too. Suddenly, as if he had just spotted something, he strode over with his broom towards the co-op, shouting, "Who's there? Who is it?"

Reaching the alley he cried with a show of surprise, "Secretary Wang! How come you slipped and fell here? Get up, quick!"

"A fine mess you've made of your sweeping. Leaving cow-dung to trip people up." Wang Qiushe was sitting in the stinking dung. Angry as he was, he dared not raise his voice.

"I'm to blame, Secretary Wang. Come on, let me help you up." Qin tugged at one of Wang's feet in the gutter.

"Ouch! That hurts! I've sprained my ankle." Wang broke out in a cold sweat.

At once Qin let go of his foot and, regardless of the filth and stench, lifted him up and sat him on the threshold.

"Well, Secretary Wang? Want to go home? Or shall I take you to the clinic?" he asked with concern.

"I'll go home. If you carry me back, Crazy Qin, I shan't forget it. Ouch...." Wang still kept his voice down for fear of waking the neighbours.

Qin bent down and hoisted Wang on to his back. The stilt-house owner seemed as strong as an ox after all these years of good living. No wonder he came out philandering at night.

"You got up too early, Secretary Wang. You must have seen a ghost to take such a tumble."

"Rubbish! Get a move on. We don't want people to see the Party secretary on the back of one of the Five Categories. . . . Presently you must go to the hills to get herbal medicine for me."

A broken bone takes a hundred days to heal. For more than two months the stilt-house owner had to keep to his bed. Luckily the brigade doctor brought him medicine and took good care of him. Li Guoxiang was too busy to find time to call. Having stayed long enough at the grassroots level she had moved back to the county.

Qin and Yuyin continued getting up at dawn to sweep the flagstone street. At first they were very happy, enjoying their daily encounters, for their triumph over Wang had drawn them closer together. They hated being apart. Each felt a longing hard to put into words. . . . One day at dusk Qin took her a flowered dacron blouse wrapped in cellophane, tied with red ribbon. Heavens, she was overwhelmed. She had never seen anything so fine. In her position she wasn't fit to wear it. After Qin left she took it out — it was as soft as silk. Not liking to put it on, she clasped it to her heart and tucked her head under the quilt to cry all night. She felt guilty, as if holding a warm heart. She decided to go and burn incense at Guigui's grave the next morning, to confide in him and ask for his advice. Guigui had always let her have her own way, had spoiled and cosseted her. His ghost would protect and forgive her; she hoped he would send her a dream. . . . The next morning when Qin knocked at her door, she had put on the dacron blouse inside her jacket, next to her heart. But she had made sure to keep even its collar hidden.

In silence they swept the street . . . then, out of the blue, Qin suddenly dropped his broom and threw his arms around her!

"Are you crazy? Heavens, Brother Qin, are you out of your mind?" Yuyin's voice trembled, her eyes brimmed with tears. . . . Sobbing, she let him hold her close and caress her. Finally she hardened her heart to push him away. How could they do such a thing? Counter-revolutionaries, the lowest of the low, how could they think of love? It just wouldn't do. . . . She hated the fire that still blazed in her heart. Why hadn't it gone out? Why couldn't she be turned into wood or stone? Everything else had been taken away. Life had put her beyond the pale as if she were a leper, and all that was left, confound it, was this tormenting fire. As she swept the street that morning tears coursed down her cheeks.

For the next few mornings they ignored each other, sweeping the street in silence. Their hearts ached. How they longed to live like real human beings. Qin still went to the inn at dawn to wait for her, turning away in silence when she came out. . . . Time can heal a wounded heart, dispel despair, quench irresistible passions. But only for a while, only on the surface.

A few weeks later Qin seemed to have calmed down. Yuyin smiled at him again, calling him "Brother Qin", and her smile and voice held a new tenderness. As if by tacit agreement they said no more about the danger they had narrowly escaped. They reverted to their old ways. Like two street-sweeping machines, they did not know why they were living or how they could live on. This situation did not last long, however. Yuyin came down with flu and ran a fever, growing delirious. Qin had to do the work of both, after which he drew on his pitiful knowledge of medicine to pick wild herbs and brew medicine for his "fellow criminal". The townsfolk no longer paid much attention to them, and so this passed unnoticed. Yuyin could only lie in bed while Qin nursed her. Every day with tears in her eyes she would falter, "Brother Qin...."

High and low have their different fates. In a couple of weeks when Yuyin had recovered she resumed her sweeping of the street. At about five every morning Qin would call her up and accompany her to the middle of the street. But this was a time of thunderstorms and high winds, for it was an unusually wet spring. They went on sweeping the street mechanically, only now they worked side by side. Suddenly a storm broke, the sky turned black and the rain came pouring down.

Yuyin tugged Qin to run back to the inn, where they arrived like drowned rats. Her room was still dark. They stripped off their drenched clothes to wring them out, and with chattering teeth she begged:

"Brother Qin... Brother Qin... do put your arms round me.... I'm freezing."

"And only just over your illness. Let me carry you to the *kang* to tuck you up snug in the quilt."

Qin groped through the dark till he was touching her. To their horror they had forgotten that they were naked.

The rain beat down, the wind roared. If only that angry thunder and lightning would stop, letting the rain and mist shut out the world! This guilty pair of political reprobates, the fire in their hearts not yet quenched, still knew the lightning of passion, the warmth of life. In the wind and rain the tree of their love burgeoned to put out delicate flowers and form bitter fruit.

## "An Intelligent Girl Like You"

It often amazed Hu Yuyin that she could endure, live on, and even fall in love with Qin Shutian. When marched back to the inn after having been struggled against, beaten and paraded, she felt life was not worth living, felt at her last gasp. Sometimes, fully dressed, she fell into a troubled sleep still wearing her black placard. Opening her eyes the next morning, she could hardly believe that she was still alive. If only she had died! She touched her breast and felt her heart still beating. That meant she must get up to sweep the street. . . .

In moments of self-pity she decided to choose a good day — the first or the fifteenth — to kill herself. As that would be her last act, she must choose a lucky day. And she mustn't spoil her looks by hanging, stabbing herself or taking ratsbane. Drowning would be best. Then, when they fished her out and laid her on a door-plank, she would seem to be sleeping, spick and span, her hair unruffled. Only her face would be white and rather puffy. Once lovely as a goddess, she should keep her good looks in death. Then her ghost would not be ugly or frightening.

So she often went up the stone bridge over Jade-leaf Stream to stare into the water. The bridge was nearly forty feet high, the stream like green silk. The moist cliffs on either side were overgrown with saxifrage and wistaria. Looking down at their reflection in the water, you could see two bridges, four cliffs. From the bridge she could see her dimples reflected in the stream. A high bridge, deep water, steep cliffs. So many unhappy women had committed suicide here that the townsfolk called it Lovelorn Bridge. Each time Yuyin came here to look at her reflection, her heart ached and she wept. Is that you, Yuyin? Are you really a bad woman? Have you wronged anyone? Have you enemies? No, none! She never trod on an ant, seldom lost her temper, never even teased children. Far from being mean or grasping, she'd helped many people. . . . So why was she persecuted, hated and struggled against? Treated as the lowest of the low, unable to hold up her head or to smile in public. It was too unfair, too cruel! "I won't die! Why should I? I've done nothing wrong, why shouldn't I live on?" So she never jumped off the bridge.

She had other ways of chastening herself. Once she fasted for three days. Yet each morning she got up to comb her hair and wash her face; each evening she had a bath and changed her clothes. On the fourth day she fainted while sweeping the street. Qin carried her back to the inn and talked to her like a brother, then made her egg soup. As he fed her he cried, the first time she had seen him in tears. When this Iron-hat Rightist was forced to kneel down on a brick or paraded with a placard, he always grinned as if going to a feast. He seemed to be an incurable optimist. Now he was crying for her — that warmed her frozen heart. She had always been soft-hearted. When Guigui was alive and they were well-off, she had dreaded hearing about other people's troubles. Qin Shutian, Crazy Qin had been protecting her. Before, she had hated him as the man responsible for her unhappiness. Hadn't he spoiled her luck by bringing all those actresses to her wedding to combat feudalism? . . . Now he was trying to make it up to her. Being in the same boat they sympathized with each other. As she lay in bed he softly sang the "Song of Copper Coins", each verse ending with "an intelligent girl like you". And as he sang he looked at her with tears in his eyes. What did he mean? He did not want her to ruin her health, he wanted her to live. Hibiscus wasn't the only place in the world, and they still had their lives before them. Besides, there must be more to life than political movements and struggles. You should realize that, an intelligent girl like you! . . .

The strains of the old folk-song which Yuyin had sung as a child made her want to live on. She began to pay more attention to Qin Shutian. One of the Five Categories, the lowest of the low, he was still so cheerful and active, as if he found nothing shameful in being labelled a monster. When publicly paraded, he always led the way boldly. At criticism meetings he flopped down on his knees, hanging his head, before being sworn at, kicked or beaten. When his left ear was boxed, he waited for another box on his right. The revolutionary masses said he wasn't a real diehard but an old campaigner. At first Yuyin had thought him contemptible. Later she came to see that he was right, because this way he got off more lightly. But she couldn't follow suit. If anyone pulled her hair, she couldn't help smoothing it. If anyone clamped down her head she always smoothed her clothes when allowed to raise it. If made to kneel, as soon as she stood up she brushed off the dust on her knees. She received extra beatings as a result, but failed to change her ways. When called "a diehard rich peasant", she wished she could die and be done with such persecution.

Something else had motivated her to live on. That was the arrival of those lawless Red Guards with their northern accent, who had pounced on Li Guoxiang the secretary of the commune and paraded her with old shoes tied round her neck. What was the world coming to — this was unheard of! It seemed anybody could be struggled against. . . . When she went home after being paraded that day, her heart was strangely light. It was bad, gloating over other people's misfortunes. She washed her face and looked at herself in the mirror, the mirror her mother had left her. Their new storeyed house, confiscated in the Four Clean-ups, had been turned into a hostel and the old inn had been left to her. It must be several years since she last looked in a mirror. She discovered she had aged, was growing wrinkled; but the contours of her face hadn't changed, her hair was still thick and soft, her eyes big and bright. It occurred to her: If Li Guoxiang weren't a cadre and I weren't a rich peasant, that bitch couldn't compare with me!

Sometimes she turned in early but couldn't sleep. It was hot and she lay naked on her quilt. She covered her eyes as if in embarrassment, then lowered her hands to her breasts, still so full and firm. Really, she was like a new bride, how disgusting, but there was nothing she could do about it. She didn't look like one of the Five Categories, who should be shrivelled and bent. After that she went on looking in the mirror, often weeping at her reflection, wishing that the fire in her heart could be extinguished.

That morning during the storm, when it was too dark to see your outstretched fingers and she and Qin were wet through, Old Man Heaven had connived at their crime. . . . But the townsfolk's vigilance was concentrated on politics and class struggle. How could they have imagined that making these two bad elements sweep the street would lead to this affair between them? Dazed and exhausted by endless movements, promotions and demotions, constant uncertainty and the slogans which changed from one day to the next, the townsfolk merely noticed that the flagstone street seemed cleaner every day, so spick and span that a grain of rice dropped by a child could be picked up and eaten. And Qin Shutian and Hu Yuyin were uncommonly diligent, volunteering for all the heaviest, dirtiest work. Yuyin's wrinkles smoothed out and her cheeks were as rosy as a flowering hibiscus. Anyone would have thought she had been notified that her "new rich peasant" label would soon be removed.

So the Iron-hat Rightist and "new rich peasant" widow lived together illicitly, in fear and trembling, like young lovers whose parents are opposed to their marriage. Yet to them every second was sweet. They embraced and kissed passionately, their long pent-up emotion finding expression at last. They knew this was very risky, in view of their political and social status. So they never lit a lamp at night, used to living in the dark and enjoying it. Sleeping on Qin's arm, sometimes in her dreams Yuyin murmured, "Guigui, Guigui." But this did not upset Qin, who would answer as if he were Guigui, still devoted to his wife. He sang Yuyin all the songs from *Wedding Songs*, and she admired his good memory, his fine voice.

"You're the one with a fine voice, Yuyin. That year I brought my actresses here, you were so charming, had such a crystal voice, that we wanted to get you to join our ensemble. But at eighteen you married. . . ."

"That was my fate. But you shouldn't have used our wedding for your rehearsal, you spoiled our luck. . . ."

"Are you crying again? I shouldn't have raked up the past."

"I don't blame you, brother. It's *my* fault, I'm ill-starred. See, I've stopped crying, sing me some more songs."

Qin sang:

My love's like a flower in bloom,
Tomorrow the sedan-chair will bring me my bride.
On red-lacquered stools, while drums and fiddles
    sound,
We'll drink in the bridal chamber side by side.

And this time she joined in, both of them singing so softly that no one outside could hear. Theirs was the happiness now of true lovers.

When summer came Yuyin suffered from nausea and could eat nothing but pickles. When at last it dawned on her that she was pregnant she nearly fainted away, not knowing whether to laugh or cry. For years she had longed in vain for a child, but now this "happy event" had caught her unawares when her life was so wretched. Why hadn't it happened earlier? If she'd had three or four children when she kept her beancurd stall, they would never have built that storeyed house. With all those extra mouths to feed she would have been eligitle for relief; and Guigui would never have taken his own life. . . . The fortune-teller had told her that she would be childless, yet here she was in the family way at last. Was this good or bad? She panicked. But she resolved to put up with any pains to have this child, even if it cost her life. People had jeered at her for being barren, and she had thought bearing children a woman's first duty.

Yuyin was in no hurry to tell Qin that she was expecting. She would wait till she was absolutely certain. But she clung to him more fondly and often cooked him special dishes which she herself would not touch. At the same time, as if purifying herself for some religious rite, she no longer slept with him, preferring to lie quietly alone without any covering, stroking her belly to feel the small life inside. . . . Her eyes shone with happiness, with tears of joy. Life had never been so good since Guigui's death. What a fool she had been to want to kill herself. How could anyone call her an intelligent girl?

One morning a month later, when positive that she was pregnant, she shared her secret with Qin. He understood then why she had treated him so affectionately yet kept him at a distance. Dropping his broom in the street he drew her to him laughing through his tears. She hastily warned him not to make a scene.

"Yuyin, we'll own up to the brigade and apply to get married," he cried, his head on her breast. "This is something I never dared dream of."

"Will they let us? Won't this count as another crime?" she answered calmly, having thought of all eventualities.

"We're still human. There's no rule forbidding the

Five Categories to marry," he assured her, his arms around her.

"If they'll let us marry, fine. But nowadays people are like mad bulls, out for blood. . . . Never mind. Don't you worry, brother. No matter what they do, this baby is ours. Oh, how I'm longing for it!"

She pressed close to him, trembling and sobbing, as if giant hands had reached out to snatch her unborn child away.

That morning, naturally, the flagstone street was not swept clean. And starting from that morning, Qin Shutian took on the duties of a husband and would not let Yuyin get up to sweep. She was able to lie in, and sometimes indulged in tantrums. Qin, whether deliberately or not, made it clear to the townsfolk that she was his woman and he would sweep her half of the street for her.

## Mortals and Devils

Wang Qiushe's fall at the foot of the co-op wall kept him indoors for two months. When Chairman Li Guoxiang came to inspect Hibiscus she visited the stilt-house and told him in a perfunctory way to take it easy and rest well, simply glancing at his badly swollen foot without touching it or showing much concern. Had she been any other woman, Wang might have sworn at her lack of sympathy. But after all their scandalous carryings-on he felt indebted to her for favouring and boosting him. For her, his superior, to visit him was an act of condescension. One could hardly expect a member of the county revolutionary committee, the chairman of the commune, to snivel or cry like an ordinary woman. Her calm showed her courage and insight. He should learn from her how to behave and get on with other people.

One day Wang, leaning on a cane, was hobbling outside the stilt-house to limber up when along came the Iron-hat Rightist. A "confession" in his hands, Qin bowed to him. Wang stopped to read the confession and gaped in astonishment, blinking.

"What the devil! Applying to marry the rich peasant widow Hu Yuyin?"

Qin bowed again and answered respectfully, "That's right, Secretary Wang." To lessen the tension he inquired politely, "Is your foot better, secretary? Shall I fetch you more herbs from the hills?"

Wang frowned, stopped blinking and narrowed his beady eyes. His feelings about this Iron-hat Rightist were mixed. When he had slipped in the cow-dung that unlucky morning, it was Qin who had carried him home and covered up for him by spreading the story that he had sprained his ankle while inspecting the paddy fields. The brigade had therefore regarded it as an injury incurred at work, and had paid for all his medical expenses. But what about Hu Yuyin? Wang had had designs on the attractive young widow, but had made no advances to her because of his affair with Li Guoxiang. Life was truly kaleidoscopic. Imagine a woman with her fine looks first marrying that dolt of a butcher, then falling into the black hands of Qin Shutian.

"Have you been having it off with her?" Wang glared at Qin as if to divine his secrets.

"Of course I can't hide the truth from you, secretary. . . ." Qin answered disarmingly with a shameless grin.

"You're farting! When did this start, eh?"

"I don't remember exactly, but I'll come clean to the higher-ups. We had to sweep the flagstone street every morning, and what with her being a widow and me a bachelor we felt drawn to each other."

"Two birds of a feather. How many times have you laid her?"

"I . . . I'd never dare, not without the higher-ups' permission."

"You're lying! Who are you fooling? A titbit like her, who's never had a child — how could a randy tomcat like you resist her?"

Qin flushed. "Don't laugh at us. Hens mate with cocks, phoenixes with phoenixes. . . . Can the brigade write us a note to take to the commune and get registered?"

Leaning on his cane Wang hobbled to a rock to sit down. He was frowning again with narrowed eyes. Qin's "confession" posed a problem. "Two of the Five Categories want to get married. . . . Is there any rule about this? The Marriage Law only mentions citizens with political rights who are over eighteen. . . . But do you count as citizens? You're the scum of society, the targets of dictatorship!"

Qin bit his lips, wiped off his smile and said grimly, "Secretary Wang, we're still human beings, aren't we? However bad, we're still human! And even if we were cocks, hens, geese or ganders, who could stop us from mating?"

Wang bellowed with laughter, tears starting to his

eyes. "Fuck your mother, Crazy Qin! I don't treat your lot like animals, that's the policy for all China, so don't you distort it. All right, I'll be lenient. We'll discuss your confession in our brigade headquarters, then send it to the commune for approval. But I'd have you know new directives have come down from the Central Committee, calling for another campaign to purify the class ranks. So you may not get permission."

Qin pleaded, "Secretary Wang, if you put in a word for us the commune will approve.... We've already ... already...."

Wang's eyes widened. He thumped the ground with his cane. "Already what? Out with it."

Qin hung his head. He decided he had better own up now rather than later. "Yuyin's in the family way...."

Wang spat in disgust. "Damned diehards! Two class enemies having it off on the sly.... Clear off! Tomorrow I'll send you a couplet on white paper to put up on the door of the inn."

The next day a militiaman delivered this couplet to Qin. It was just what he wanted. Smiling all over his face he took it to the inn. Yuyin, lighting the fire, burst into tears at the sight.

Putting up white couplets was a punishment introduced during the movement to do away with old ideas, old customs and the old culture, to make public the scandalous goings-on of lovers, so that their names stank.

"Don't cry, Yuyin. See what's written here? It won't hurt us." He spread out the couplet. "Our relationship is publicly acknowledged by the brigade,

A guilty pair
A black couple.

And above is: The Monsters' Lair. Who cares whether
we're black or white or labelled as monsters. The brigade's made it clear that we are husband and wife."

Qin was really a clever devil. Yuyin stopped crying.
With her approval he made some paste and stuck the
white couplet neatly on the inn gate.

Word of this caused a great stir in Hibiscus.  Old
and young came to marvel at this wonder.

"A black couple — that's a fact."

"Yes, a widow in her thirties, a bachelor in his forties, just right for each other!"

"Will they give a wedding feast?"

"If they do, who'd dare go?"

"Is this some kind of retribution?"

For half a month the townsfolk could talk of nothing else. Gu Yanshan, still nominally the deputy
manager of the grain depot, went to look at the couplet
but did not make any comment.

The townsfolk's speculations gave Qin and Yuyin an
idea. One evening when all the shops were closed, they
prepared two bottles of wine and a dozen dishes, put
their wine cups on red paper as if for some ritual, then
raised these nuptial cups. Though the commune had not
given its approval, no one was likely to take any interest
in their wedding.  If they did, that would be showing
them a favour. Anyway it was already a fait accompli,
accepted by the brigade and their fellow townsfolk.
Like attracts like. If two monsters came together it
didn't hurt anyone else. Their faces shone with joy. . . .

As they toasted each other in the time-honoured way

they heard knocking at the gate. It terrified them. Yu-yin trembled and Qin put his arm round her to protect her. Knock, knock, knock!

Qin whispered, "Listen to that knocking. It's not the way the militia come to nab us, yelling their heads off and kicking the door or pounding it with rifle butts. . . ."

Yuyin calmed down and nodded. Men kept their heads in a crisis.

"Shall I open the door?" he asked.

"Yes."

When Qin summoned up courage to open the door, he discovered that it was Old Gu, the "soldier from the north". He had brought a cardboard box and a gourd of liquor. Well, this was a surprise! Qin hastily asked him in and bolted the door while Yuyin, still pale with fright, offered him a seat. And Old Gu did not stand on ceremony.

"Earlier today I spotted you buying fish and pork on the sly. . . . I thought, I must go and drink a cup at their wedding. . . . I figured you wouldn't report me. . . . You two, as far as I can see, aren't the usual run of the Five Categories. And a marriage comes only once — or at most twice in a lifetime. . . ."

When the "black couple" heard this, tears streamed from their eyes and they knelt down to kowtow. So in this world of cut-throats there were still decent people. Sympathy and kindness hadn't died out completely.

Gu Yanshan let them kowtow to him. Then chuckling rather tipsily he said, "Get up, get up. This is the old-fashioned way. Want me to act as go-between? These last few years, looking at the world with drunken eyes, I see everything more clearly. Actually your go-betweens

were your brooms and the flagstones in the street. . . .
Never mind, this evening I can play the part!"

Husband and wife wanted to kneel again, but he
hastily made them sit down as if he were really the
master of ceremonies.

"I've brought you a small present." Old Gu opened
the cardboard box and took out four lengths of cloth,
a toy car and aeroplane and a doll. "Don't refuse now.
I give presents like this whenever any of the townsfolk
marry. . . . Hope you'll soon have a bouncing son . . .
doesn't matter whether you're red or black, now that
you're married you're bound to have children."

Yuyin felt so overwhelmed she nearly fainted away
. . . but she took a grip on herself. Kneeling before Old
Gu again she sobbed:

"Chairman Gu! You must let me kneel to you. . . .
Because of me and those rice seconds, you were fram-
ed. . . . I'm to blame for all your troubles . . . and you
an old cadre from the north. . . . If all cadres, all Party
members were like you, we'd have some peace. . . .
Chairman Gu, if you don't despise me, I'll slave like
an ox to make it up to you."

That reduced Old Gu to tears too, but he forced a
smile. "Get up, get up, let's enjoy ourselves, why harp
on that? We're the ones who know ourselves best. Come
on, drink! There's no work for me now in the grain
depot, so this evening I mean to get good and drunk."
Qin reset the table. Husband and wife toasted Old
Gu with brimming glasses of wine. But having tossed
his back he produced his gourd, making them regret not
having bought a bottle of spirits that day.

"That sweet red wine will make you a loving couple.
But I'll stick to my fire-water — more kick in it."

They toasted each other in turn, all deeply moved. Then Gu proposed, "Old Qin! I heard you were made a Rightist because of some wedding songs, and Yuyin has a fine voice, so why not sing now at your own wedding feast?"

How could they refuse this request? Flushed with wine and happiness, husband and wife struck up the lively *Chair-bearer's Song*:

> Why cry, pretty bride? We'll carry you there,
> Our eyes your lanterns, our shoulders your chair.
> Four men, eight legs fly like the wind,
> Our shoulders sore, the bend and slope left be-
> hind.
> Give me a smile, a laugh; I'll quench my thirst
> At your wedding feast, but call me "brother" first!

A month later Qin Shutian and Hu Yuyin were sum moned to the commune. They thought it was to register their marriage; but Qin took the precaution of taking along two changes of clothes in a bag.

As soon as they entered the office, Chairman Li Guoxiang pounded her desk and thundered at Qin:

"Qin Shutian! Of all the gall, you Iron-hat Rightist!"

Wang Qiushe was sitting beside her, his face furious. With them was another commune cadre, paper and pen before him.

Qin and Yuyin lowered their heads, their arms at their sides. Not knowing what was wrong Qin said, "I admit my crime to the leadership. . . ."

"When labouring under surveillance, in defiance of the laws and of the masses you lived in sin with the rich peasant Hu Yuyin, making a frenzied attack on the proletarian dictatorship...."

The previous evening, when Wang Qiushe had come to ask for instructions, Chairman Li had pressed him for details about his sprained ankle. He described how he had slipped in some cow-dung while leaving the co-op first thing in the morning and how Qin, then sweeping the street, had carried him back to the stilt-house. Recently, he said, Qin's conduct had improved.

"Trust you to be taken in!" she jeered. "You fool! How wide is that alley by the co-op's side gate? People never lead cows down it. How could cow-dung come there? You spent so many nights in the co-op, the Iron-hat Rightist must have spotted you and laid that trap for you! Dumb as an ox you are, with no notion of class struggle!"

Wang wished he could hide his head for shame. But he was convinced — she had better judgement than he did.

"Class revenge! Tomorrow I'll send militiamen to nab Crazy Qin! I'll have his hide!" Wang was livid at having been tricked and made to suffer for over two months by a Rightist.

"We mustn't use force, mustn't flay a class enemy," she answered calmly. "Hasn't he asked to marry Hu Yuyin? In fact they're living together openly. First we'll announce that their marriage is illegal. Then send him to a labour camp for ten years — we can notify the county authorities. In a labour camp he won't be able to spy on us." So Qin and Yuyin were summoned to the commune.

"Qin Shutian! Hu Yuyin! Is it true that you are co-habiting illicitly?" Li Guoxiang demanded sternly.

Qin looked up to plead, "I've done wrong. . . . But we handed in a confession to the brigade cadres and they sent us a white paper couplet acknowledging us as a 'black couple'. . . . We thought, seeing that she was a widow and I was a bachelor of over forty, both in the Five Categories, and we hadn't done anything sneaky . . . the commune leadership would give permission. . . ."

"You're farting!" Hearing this insinuation Wang pounded the desk and sprang to his feet. "You shameless swine! Rightist hooligan! Counter-revolutionary scoundrel! Kneel to beg my pardon, quick! Today I've seen through you, you dog. Dammit, kneel!"

Yuyin took Qin's arm. A Rightist for so many years, today for the first time he refused to kneel or even hang his head. In the past he had submitted to political orders, but he wasn't going to kneel to this lecher. Yuyin, sensing this, plucked up courage. Wang charged towards them fiercely brandishing his huge fists.

"Wang Qiushe! Let me say a word before you kill us!" Yuyin faced up firmly to the stilt-house owner, and the look in her eyes halted him.

"How long have we known each other? This isn't the first time we've stood face to face, is it? But I've never washed your dirty linen in public. . . . I won't in future either. All the townsfolk know about us and accept our relationship, and we long ago asked permission to register. So today just tell me this: Are we the ones who've broken the law, or those cadres who make reports in the daytime and sneak through side gates after dark?"

"How dare you! Open defiance!" Even seasoned Li Guoxiang had lost her cool. She began to swear like a fishwife: "Diehard rich peasant! Slut! Bitch! ... I'll tear out your tongue!"

This scene was a disgrace to the commune office. The art of struggle, dignified leadership, a high political level had all been flung to the winds. But now Chairman Li gritted her teeth and took a grip on herself, clenching her fists. She had learned from Vice-commander Lin Biao that political power is the power of repression. The time had come to exercise this power.

"Send in some militiamen! Bring wire! Strip the rich peasant woman naked and wire her breasts!"

Were these inhuman orders carried out? It does not bear writing about. But even more primitive tortures than these were carried out in China in the late sixties of the twentieth century.

When the new movement to purify the class ranks was launched in the commune, Qin and Yuyin were its chief targets as counter-revolutionary criminals. Their trial took place on the stage in Hibiscus market-place. Qin was sentenced to ten years' hard labour and Yuyin to three; but she, being pregnant, would not be sent to a camp. Many of the townsfolk shed tears for them in secret, including Li Mangeng and his wife Peppery. These townsfolk had no firm stand and could not distinguish between friend and foe. They failed to realize that any kindness to unarmed enemies like Qin Shutian would have endangered the people. That if they were to stage a come-back, tens of thousands of revolutionary heads would fall, streams of blood would flow and corpses would strew the ground. Then Qin would put on his *Wedding Songs* again, attacking socialism as if it were feudalism, and their country would change colour. Yuyin would set up her stall again, selling beancurd at ten cents a bowl to exploit the people, so that she could build another storeyed house and become a new landlord or a new rich peasant.

Qin and Yuyin proved stubborn and defiant at their trial. They shed no tears. All these years of being struggled against had turned them into unregenerate diehards, the social base of counter-revolutionary revisionism. Qin refused to admit his guilt or bow his head. And Yuyin held herself proudly, letting everybody see the vile new life she was carrying. Even when sentence was passed, the militiamen could not clamp down the prisoners' heads.

Standing side by side, they looked into each other's eyes. They said not a word, that would not have been allowed. But each knew what the other diehard was thinking.

"Live on, just stick it out."

"Don't worry. Most of the townsfolk are good people. I shall stick it out for our child."

# Part 4
# The New Mood of the People
## (1979)

## Hibiscus River and Jade-Leaf Stream

Time is a river, a river of life, flowing through men's memories. It flows slowly, silently, glinting. But who knows how it wells up through the cracks in granite? Despite all the obstacles put in its way, it presses steadily onwards, twisting and turning. It plunges over sheer cliffs into abysses, throwing up clouds of mist. Then it gathers its strength again to surge forward with roars of defiance, proclaiming that no force on earth can hold it back. Monkeys can drink its water, deer bathe in it, herons preen their plumage, poisonous snakes dart through it, and wild beasts fight on its shores. Men punt their rafts along it, build vast dams to generate hydroelectric power. None of this will stop it from flowing on to the great ocean.

Life is a river of happiness and grief, beset by dangers yet endlessly fascinating. All manner of people play their different parts and strike their different poses. Wives denounce their husbands; sons accuse their fathers; the best of friends turn into deadly foes. Virtues turn into vices: humanity and human warmth are labelled bourgeois. Mass movements move the masses, till those pulling the strings become a target themselves.

How can the earth stop rotating? We must fight to the bitter end. In the struggle for power how can everyone survive? If Rightists didn't stink, how could Leftists smell sweet? The unprecedented "cultural revolution" saw a huge swing to the Left, and nets had to be spread everywhere to capture the Rightist devils. Documents, reports, endless meetings large and small and frenzied political movements were all to wipe out what was bourgeois and foster what was proletarian. It was bourgeois to grow pumpkins or paprikas by your cottage. You should grow sunflowers facing the glorious sun, but were not allowed to crack and eat their seeds. Who said there were no capitalists? A stallholder could develop into one. Private plots and free markets were hotbeds of capitalism which must be attacked, for capitalism should be wiped out in its cradle before reaching disastrous dimensions. If every household sold paprikas or pumpkins, which could be made into liquor, wouldn't the collective's fields go untilled? So paprikas and pumpkins were threats. If everyone had money and lived better than landlords before Liberation, with plenty to eat every day, who would make revolution? What would happen to the class ranks? Who would the cadres going down to the grassroots rely on? The poor and lower-middle peasants should always remain the majority. If they became rich that would cause complete confusion. China had endless problems, being an ocean of bourgeoisie and petty-bourgeoisie. The key for these problems was to have fierce struggles every few years. This was magnificent and became habit-forming. Yes, struggle was the key, their national treasure. But it was no substitute for

Marxism. Social changes were determined by ruthless historical laws. In October 1976,* history imprinted a big exclamation mark on China's sacred soil. This was followed by a series of big question marks. The Third Plenary Session of the Party saved the country from disaster. The ice was broken; the river of life raced on exultantly.

It should be noted that even during the days of blind adherence to the ultra-Left line, the river of life flowed on. There was progress in Hibiscus tucked away in the Wuling Mountains. A bridge for motor traffic was built and a new highway for carts, tractors, trucks and buses. Occasionally a jeep drove along it which the children of Hibiscus chased after, wide-eyed, knowing that Deputy Secretary Li Guoxiang of the county revolutionary committee must have come back to her "base" to inspect the work. Some factories were started. A paper mill to make use of the inexhaustible supply of bamboo. A distillery making spirits out of cassava, the roots of kudzu vine and grain. An ironworks and a small power station. The population of the town more than doubled. And so there appeared a bus station, hospital, inns, shops selling soft drinks, hairdressers, tailors, a Xinhua Bookstore, a post and telegraph office. ... A new road intersecting the market-place was called New Street, while the flagstone street became Old Street.

Hibiscus had its revolutionary committee and local government, which overlapped to some extent with the commune. The revolutionary committee's chairman was Wang Qiushe. Under the committee were a police station, a broadcasting station and several other sections.

---

* The time of the arrest of the "gang of four".

So the place though small was a going concern. The police station was in charge of every household, of checking profiteering and training the militia. It had dealt with many "reactionary slogans". Some loudspeakers were fixed up in New and Old Streets, and later each household put up a square box which three times a day relayed model operas and revolutionary songs, the announcements of the revolutionary committee and local news. There was plenty of local news, all highly political. Earlier on there had been the campaigns to repudiate Lin Biao and Confucius and to praise the Legalists, to exercise complete dictatorship over the bourgeoisie, and to publicize the achievements of Hibiscus in the "cultural revolution"; then there had been the campaign to repudiate Deng Xiaoping and the Right-deviationist plot to reverse correct verdicts. Now the woman announcer was exposing the heinous crimes of Lin Biao and the "gang of four", denouncing their ultra-Left line and the ten years of turmoil. She explained the tasks of this new period and called for a new Long March to modernize China. Her broadcasts drowned out all other sounds, including the din of the traffic and the factories. Neighbours hardly able to hear each other speak stopped confiding in each other, and this was good for public security.

These developments were naturally accompanied by new problems. The traffic on the highway raised clouds of dust which hung in the air like a pall. Old Street was not so bad, but the buildings on New Street were smothered in dust which could only be washed away by heavy rain. As New Street had no sewers, people emptied their slops on the dirt road. In fine weather the soil could absorb it, but on rainy days the road was a mass of puddles, and truck drivers spattered mud over all the buildings and windows. Well, that saved folk the trouble of putting up curtains. When Wang Qiushe and his colleagues had planned New Street's construction, they had forgotten sewage. Urged to remedy this, Wang said, "What do we need sewage for? We can have a gutter. We don't want to westernize like Guangzhou or Shanghai." All the Five Categories were given a deadline, ordered to dig a gutter.

There were contradictions between different factories. Most of them were built by the river, where it was easy to pump up or drain away water, or ship out their products by boat. They dumped waste into it too. The paper mill, though four-*li* away from the distillery on Jadeleaf Stream, hadn't foreseen the trouble of pollution. When they started discharging alkaline water into the stream, which flowed down to Hibiscus River, that gave a bitter taste to the distillery's liquor. The distillers complained to high heaven and demanded damages, whereupon the paper mill urged them to move away. The case was taken to the county for arbitration, but the county referred it to the Hibiscus Revolutionary Committee. What could Wang Qiushe do? The town could not afford to move the distillery. For fear that some workers would fight and maybe get killed, he rushed to the county town to beg Secretary Yang Min'gao and Deputy Secretary Li Guoxiang to organize a study class for the factory managers. Finally they adopted the "Doctrine of the Mean" of Confucius whom they had repudiated. With the paper mill supplying funds, the distillery labour, a cement pipe was laid to bring in clear water from the hills three *li* away.

Of course behind the backs of both secretaries the two factory heads came to a tacit agreement: the cadres of the paper mill would be allowed to buy liquor at cut prices from the distillery.

And what of Hibiscus River and Jade-leaf Stream with their pea-green water, their verdant banks? Already the townsfolk were up in arms about this. However, it had not yet been put on the revolutionary committee's agenda. Because of all the industrial waste in the water, no vegetation grew on the cliffs, which were crumbling. And refuse was choking the channels, enlarging the banks, which were being enclosed as new fields. White alkaline bubbles floated on the placid water. Hibiscus had once been known for its red carp, but now not even many prawns or crabs were left.

Some averred: Pollution is a by-product of modernization. The advanced industrial countries of the first and second world all went through this phase. According to the news a few years earlier, there was hardly a sparrow left in Japan or America. England had to import oxygen. So how could Hibiscus, tucked away in the interior of China, a third-world country, steer clear of pollution? Anyway they still had sparrows and oxygen. Indeed, sparrows were such a pest that in early summer the commune members put scarecrows in the wheat fields to scare them away. If science and democracy went together, feudalism and ignorance were the attendants of Buddha. After repudiating capitalism for over twenty years it had dawned on them that capitalism was more advanced than feudalism; in fact deeprooted feudalism had been attacking new-fledged socialism.

# Li Guoxiang's Transfer

A few years before this a prestigious university in Beijing had planned to set up a department of class struggle as an unparalleled feat in the revolutionization of education. Evidently they couldn't see the wood for the trees. For class struggle had long been the main course for the whole country, and schooling in it had taken many forms, its students ranging from old to young. Virtually all our cadres were trained or steeled in this school by means of bitter soul-searching and sedulous study.

A few years earlier, a woman leader in Beijing had tried to follow in the steps of Lü Zhi, Wu Zetian and the Empress Dowager Cixi. During the campaign to repudiate Lin Biao and Confucius she stressed the need to train able women successors. "What's so wonderful about you men?" she demanded. "You just have an extra prick." This showed her thoroughgoing materialism. Her favour was extended throughout the country, manifested in all revolutionary committees. And so Li Guoxiang, the secretary of the commune, was made the woman secretary of the county committee. Not that this was such a very high position. Many women of her age and experience were provincial heads whose names were frequently broadcast and whose photographs appeared in the newspapers. One even became a deputy premier and while speaking to a Japanese medical delegation made the gaffe of asking, "Has Comrade Li Shizhen* come back yet from the cadre school?" All these women

---

* 1518-1593, a famous Chinese physician who wrote *Materia Medica*.

officials had been trained in class struggle. So had Li Guoxiang had access to the Forbidden City, she too might have been made a deputy premier.

But promotion had not come easily to her. She had had to adjust herself to stormy upheavals. She was now the wife of a middle-aged leading cadre in the provincial capital, a man widowed at the start of the "cultural revolution". They were still living apart, for she hoped to make quicker progress by a few more years of tempering at the grassroots. At a meeting of county cadres after the fall of the "gang of four", her denunciation of their ultra-Left line and the crimes of their followers brought tears to many eyes. She, a cadre in her thirties, secretary of the commune, had actually been lumped together with the Five Categories and paraded with all those monsters, a black placard and old shoes hung round her neck. She had been forced to do heavy physical labour building a bridge, yet when she asked for more rice and couldn't dance a "black devil's dance", they had forced her to crawl like a dog. This filled her hearers' hearts with indignation. What a way to treat a good woman Party member!... Of course, she had been wrong to speak of "Leftists suppressing a Leftist". The "Leftists" of that faction had been fascists whereas she was a genuine revolutionary, utterly different in nature. And when she had ordered the breasts of the new rich peasant Hu Yuyin to be wired, she had been prompted by righteous indignation. One could show no mercy to class enemies. Naturally she did not say this at the meeting, as it had nothing to do with the "gang of four". Besides, who didn't sometimes go to extremes? Even the revolutionary teachers were men, not gods; so of course she, Li Guoxiang, was only human.

After the Third Plenary Session of the Party's Eleventh Congress, the county committee put her in charge of righting all wrong verdicts in the county, rehabilitating Rightists, and changing the status of landlords and rich peasants. As women always paid careful attention to detail, she seemed suited to this task. Of course injustices should be set right. All those unjustly killed must have their names cleared, and work should be found for their families. It was easy to understand how in 1957 certain cadres who expressed wrong views had been labelled Rightists; but they were not class enemies, and now that they had been re-educated all they had to do was adopt the right attitude to the Party. Modernization needed science and culture, so why shouldn't use be made of intellectuals?

As for taking off the labels of landlords and rich peasants and improving their children's status, this was too much for Li Guoxiang. Who would be the revolution's target in future? Who could be used as negative examples? Without taking class struggle as the key how could they run the countryside? What could they say at meetings? To throw away class struggle was like a blind man throwing away his cane. Was all the experience gained in thirty years of political movements now obsolete? To be scrapped? Would they have to start from scratch, racking their brains and studying agricultural techniques and factory management? This made no appeal to her. Indeed, she felt an instinctive aversion to the idea, afraid that it spelt regression. In the daytime she hid her feelings, but at night in her sleep she gnashed her teeth.

Li Guoxiang's judgement was based on her own experience, position and interests. Her uncle, Secretary Yang Min'gao, soon noticed this unhealthy tendency. One evening he talked to her like a father.

"Well? Do you have doubts about the Party's line and policy? Wavering, are you? Can't keep in step with the new policy? That won't do. The history of our Party's two-line struggle proves that cadres who can't adjust to each major change in tactics are bound to be eliminated by the Party and the age. Haven't you seen many such cases? You've been given the task of carrying out this policy, so don't let yourself be swayed by personal feelings. We must always obey the Party. We are low-ranking cadres, not policy-makers. Even if this decision is later considered a mistake, the responsibility won't be ours. We're a long way from the centre of power. We just carry out instructions. That applies to rehabilitating landlords and rich peasants and improving their children's status. We can always label them again if we're told to. Come what may we must be loyal to the Party."

Well, her uncle knew all about the rules of struggle. Only people with such a high level could swim freely in the sea of politics. This was how he came to be deputy secretary of the prefectural Party committee and first secretary of the county committee. She wasn't up to him, wasn't fully seasoned. That was why she was still only a deputy secretary of the county committee. But one day she would learn to swim freely too.

Yang Min'gao was annoyed and worried by his niece's failure to comply with this new change of line. She was too set in her ideas! As her superior and uncle he saw further and took the whole situation into account. There had recently been more talk in the county committee about his niece's affair with Wang Qiushe. It wasn't good for her to live too long apart from her husband. He should point this out to his nephew-in-law and together they could pull strings to get her transferred to the provincial capital. Then when she came down again to inspect the work she would have a higher status — what was wrong with that? He insinuated this to his niece, who was quick to grasp his reasoning.

As soon as she went to her office the next morning, Li Guoxiang looked at the files dealing with cases of injustice from the security bureau. She took out the one on "Qin Shutian, wrongly labelled a Rightist in 1957, now a criminal in custody" and on "Hu Yuyin, wrongly labelled a new rich peasant in 1964". These two sheaves of material weighed heavily in her hands. She picked them up, put them down, picked them up again, unable to make up her mind. She twiddled her pen, which felt as heavy as iron. How was it that this pen, with its power over life and death, sometimes raced over the paper like a dragon, at others dried up and lost its incisiveness? She fiddled with it for a while without writing a single word. Then decided that first she would ring up Hibiscus to put Wang Qiushe in the picture.

"What? Clear them? Rehabilitate them both?" Wang bellowed furiously over the phone. "I don't get it! I'm dead against it! When you chop and change up there, there's the devil to pay down here!"

## Mayor Wang

"Fuck it! A damn fool they've made of me! What face, what prestige will I have left in Hibiscus?"

Wang Qiushe was used to being addressed as "mayor", not knowing that behind his back the townsfolk referred to him as the Autumn Snake. There was no silencing people's dirty talk. Although Secretary Li Guoxiang had rung him up to notify him that Qin Shutian and Hu Yuyin were to be rehabilitated, when instructions to this effect came from the county he flew into a rage. Shutting himself up in his office he pounded his desk, so that his glass crashed on to the cement floor.

He was wrong, of course, to blame Li Guoxiang. How could someone in her low position block the Central Committee's directives, which had shaken the land like spring thunder, to right the wrongs done in previous political movements?

Li Guoxiang knew how Wang would react, for though their affair had ended they still felt close to each other. He could have found himself a wife, but because of his devotion to her all these years he had gone without a family of his own. Just for this she was grateful to him. So a few days later she rang him up again to talk him round. As it was a special line, the exchange operator dared not listen in and no one knew what was said. But after receiving this call Wang flopped back in his wicker chair, his forehead wet with cold sweat. This time he did not shut the door, pound his desk or smash a glass. But inwardly he was fuming:

"Shit! Clear them, take off their caps, treat them as targets of dictatorship within the ranks of the people.... It's all very well to talk like that, but you're shitting on me and expect me to lick your arse! You're sitting pretty, going to work in the province, leaving me in the lurch here to right all wrongs.... You've chosen the best way out. Go on, go. You and me, a hen and a gander, can't sleep together long."

Wang's affair with Li Guoxiang had benefited them both. Each had gained and also lost out. So why complain? Besides he had gained more than he lost. A muddy-footed oaf, he was now the mayor of Hibiscus. All thanks to the boosting given him by Li Guoxiang and Secretary Yang Min'gao. Had it been left to Yang, he would never have promoted a lout like Wang, a nobody who kept backsliding. Take the case of Li Mangeng. Because he hadn't listened to Yang in 1956, he was doomed to wear straw sandals and a coir cape all his life. How about Wang Qiushe then? His moral character and ability were nowhere near as good as Li's. But an incident just before the Spring Festival during the campaign to denounce Lin Biao and Confucius had made Yang revise his impression of him completely.

Yang Min'gao's whole family, the secretary himself in particular, loved to eat winter bamboo shoots. They couldn't do without those succulent crisp shoots fried with lean pork, braised with chicken or duck, stewed with mushrooms, and crunched them with an indescribable relish. Besides, bamboo shoots grew in the mountains and weren't such rareties as swallow-nests, silver mushrooms, sea slugs or bear's paws; so what was wrong with a county head eating a couple of hundred pounds of them in winter and spring? Unfortunately that year all the bamboos flowered, then withered. Winter bamboo shoots became as rare as shark's fin. One evening Li Guoxiang hinted to Wang that here was his chance to prove his loyalty and win promotion. The next day there was a market in Hibiscus and, with her tacit consent, on the pretext of suppressing speculation and upholding public order he sent militiamen to clamp down on it. As it was just before the Spring Festival, the commune members had brought in mountain products. To their surprise they were allowed to take them in but not to take them out. They were searched by militiamen in yellow armbands, and all the winter bamboo shoots in their crates were confiscated. Nothing else was taken though. No one could query this — it was a top secret. The pedlars looked at each other in dismay.

Then someone claiming to be in the know spread word that a reactionary gang, the Bamboo Shoot Party, had been found in the mountains. Its members hid secret messages in bamboo shoots. So a trap had been laid for them, and there was no telling how many of their ringleaders and followers would be caught at this market. The pedlars whose bamboo shoots were confiscated did not mind the financial loss. They only wished they could grow wings to fly home where they could live quietly all the year round; stirring out landed them in trouble.

Who made up the top secret about the Bamboo Shoot Party? Was it some militiaman who wanted to embarrass Mayor Wang? Or someone at the market? At all events Wang and Li Guoxiang exchanged worried glances, afraid the business might be blown up and exposed. They held meetings large and small to scotch this rumour and assert that this search of the market had simply been to clamp down on speculators. So the trouble was smoothed over.

But to return to the night of that market in Hibiscus. Wang Qiushe put the precious bamboo shoots — over a hundred pounds of them — in two sacks, tied them on his bicycle and rode sixty *li* in the dark to the county town to deliver them to Secretary Yang's kitchen. Not a soul knew about this. When Yang discovered them first thing the next morning, he knitted his brows and read Wang Qiushe a lecture. This was no way to show respect and consideration for his superiors. Giving away local products was a vulgar, unhealthy tendency. It was wrong for those in leading positions to have special privileges. He even linked these two sacks of bamboo shoots with understanding of the Party line and the prevention of revisionism. He made Wang weigh them with him, then worked out their cost, but for the time being did not pay him. Wang's heart sank. He blamed Li Guoxiang for misleading him, not relaxing till Yang said, "Well, don't do this again. Watch your step." Thereupon he invited him to breakfast, a simple meal of steamed buns, soy milk, preserved eggs, strong-smelling beancurd and a saucer of white sugar. During this meal Yang asked Wang about his work and his living conditions — had he any difficulties? Of course Wang made no mention of that damaging rumour about a Bamboo Shoot Party, so Yang knew nothing about it. All he knew was that winter bamboo shoots grew in the mountains, and when the peasants dug them up with their hoes that affected the growth of the bamboos in spring.

Before long Li Guoxiang was recalled to the county, where she gave Yang a detailed report on the commune cadres. This naturally included an account of Brigade Secretary Wang Qiushe, his repentance and progress in the last few years, and his loyalty to his superiors. As Yang of course did not believe in damning a man for a single mistake, he forgave Wang for parroting the charges against him in the early days of the "cultural revolution". His subsequent behaviour was more important. Some days later word went round Hibiscus that to train and give responsibility to grassroots cadres who had a firm stand, the county committee was promoting Wang to be deputy chairman of the commune committee. But the truth will out, the road to happiness is strewn with setbacks. Someone denounced Wang Qiushe to the provincial authorities for confiscating those bamboo shoots. Who was the informer? The crowd at the market that day had been very mixed with all kinds of different backgrounds and social connections. Impossible to investigate them all. According to the current normal procedure, indictments sent by the masses to the provincial heads had to be sent down to the district and the county, then to the commune concerned. So this one ended up in Li Guoxiang's hands, with the recommendations, "Please investigate and deal with this case", "Handle this according to the relevant Party policies" or "Let the commune deal with this". Different dates had been written on each, the round seals of authority varied in size and some were brighter than others.

This indictment had some effect. For the time being the county committee did not authorize the district to promote Wang. Even Secretary Yang could only shake his head and sigh over the stubborn way in which diehards kept down newly emerging forces. Later, when the situation had changed, the county committee decided to designate Hibiscus as a small town one degree smaller than a commune, and to appoint Wang Qiushe chairman of its revolutionary committee, still earning workpoints and drawing a subsidy. Since this came un-

der the county's jurisdiction they did not have to get
it approved higher up. If Wang steeled himself well at
the grassroots level his prospects were excellent. . . .

"Shit! Were we wrong to struggle for over twenty
years? Now they say Crazy Qin should never have been
convicted, never made a Rightist in 1957! He's to be
released and given back his old job! He'll be earning
much more than me — the mayor. . . . And Secretary
Yang is selling me short. I've run this place for years
yet I'm still not on the state pay-roll, still earning workpoints with only a subsidy of thirty-six yuan a month
. . . ."

In the office of the revolutionary committee Wang
stared blankly at the files of Qin and Yuyin, unable to
make up his mind. Rehabilitate them or not? Use de-
laying tactics? But each day the papers and radio an-
nouncers reported cases of injustice righted throughout
the country. What could the mayor of a small town do?

"Fuck them! This means Crazy Qin will no longer
be a Rightist or Hu Yuyin a rich peasant; the head
of the co-op will be reinstated, the head of the tax-
office cleared . . . and Gu Yanshan that 'soldier from
the north'. They'll all be cleared. Who hasn't made some
mistakes up here in the mountains in the last twenty-
odd years? Gu Yanshan seems to have done less badly
than the rest. And if not for all our struggles year after
year, would I have climbed up to my present post? I'd
still be a nobody, the stilt-house owner. You have to see
both sides."

What worried him most, however, was an urgent
financial problem. They would have to return that
storeyed house confiscated when Hu Yuyin was declared a rich peasant. They had long ago stopped using

it for their Class Struggle Exhibition and turned it into a hostel. That small hostel brought in a hundred yuan or more a month, tax-free. When the higher-ups came to inspect their work, or when friendly units came to co-operate with them, this sum was used to feast them. "We'll explain this to Hu Yuyin and ask her to be public-spirited. The property rights of the house will be hers, but we'll go on using it for the time being as a hostel, paying her a few dollars rent. That shouldn't be a big problem."

Another more pressing problem was how to return Hu Yuyin the one thousand five hundred confiscated from her. After all these years that money had melted away. To start with he'd had no subsidy; later on he got only thirty-six yuan a month, not nearly enough for food, drink, sundry expenses and presents for different people. It was not as if he could print notes for himself!

"Shit! Where's that money to come from? Leave it in arrears? That's right, just stall. All these years of political movements have messed up the economy. . . . Who was that money given to first? Was there any receipt? Hell no! No account was kept. . . . Hu Yuyin, the Party and government have cleared you, given you back your status as a small trader as well as your storeyed house, and allowed you to live lawfully with Qin Shutian — what more do you want?"

Still, Wang found it harder and harder to muddle along. All sorts of talk was going round the town, all detrimental to him. It was said that the higher-ups were going to make the "soldier from the north" the Party secretary and chairman of their revolutionary committee. No official announcement of this had yet come down, but already the townsfolk were gloating. Wang was not such a fool that he did not realize this. He felt a sword was hanging over his head. And he could no longer call meetings to investigate and debunk rumours. He had rung up the county committee several times to find out the situation, but was always given an evasive answer. His thoughts in a whirl, he was off his food, couldn't sleep soundly. He sat woodenly in his office, his face rather puffy, his eyes fixed, muttering incoherently. His mind was so confused that one day he bellowed:

"I won't stand for it! So long as I'm in power, don't expect to be cleared, to be rehabilitated!"

## Gu Yanshan As Foster-Father

During the years of turmoil when people accused, sold out and destroyed each other or tried to save their own skins, morality, kindness and integrity did not die out but simply took different forms. Gu Yanshan the "soldier from the north" viewed the world with tipsy eyes. When Qin Shutian was sent to a labour camp and Hu Yuyin ordered to work under supervision, Old Gu had been jittery for some days, having acted as go-between for that black couple. However, they proved to have some fellow-feeling and to be trustworthy: they did not report him or let him in for another investigation. If they had he would have lost his post and his Party membership.

One evening towards the end of that year, a howling north wind was whirling down big snowflakes when Old Gu, tipsy again, passed the old inn. He heard groans from inside and heart-rending cries, "Oh, mother, help. . . . This is killing me!" His hair stood on end. "Has Yuyin's time come?" he wondered. At once he mounted the steps, shook off the snow on his boots and coat and tried the door. It wasn't bolted. Groping his way through the pitch-black hall he made for a little room which had been partitioned off. There, by the dim light of an oil lamp he saw Yuyin lying on her bed clutching desperately at the bed-posts, her face beaded with sweat and almost fainting with pain. The shock sobered Old Gu, who had never seen such a sight.

"Yuyin, you, are you near your time?"

"Chairman Gu, do help me . . . help me to sit up and give me a drink. . . ."

Old Gu shivered, sorry that he had come in. He managed to find some warm water for Yuyin to drink, and she asked him for a towel to wipe her sweat. Then she caught hold of him like a drowning woman clinging to a rock.

"Chairman Gu, you've saved my life. . . . I'm thirty-three . . . that's old for the first baby."

"I'll go and fetch a midwife." Old Gu was sweating too with desperation.

"No, no, have a heart . . . don't leave me! . . . The women in town spit at me. I'm scared of them. . . . Do stay with me, I'll soon be dead anyway. Me and the baby, we're done for. . . . Oh, mother, why did you leave me to go through this! . . ."

"Don't cry, Yuyin. Stick it out. If it hurts, just yell . . . ."

His heart ached for her. Compassion gave him the courage to do his best to save mother and child. What if she was a new rich peasant — bah! Wasn't there an old saying: Saving someone in danger is better than building a pagoda for Buddha? At worst he could only be reprimanded and punished. His mind made up, he took heart.

"Don't you worry, Yuyin. I'll do what I can. . . ."

"You've saved my life. . . . If only all the cadres sent by the government were like you. . . . You're so good, coming to my rescue. . . . With you here I may pull through. . . . Boil a pan of water, will you, and make me some egg soup. . . . I haven't had a bite to eat all day. They say a woman in labour should eat to keep up her strength. . . ."

As briskly as he had obeyed orders to charge when a guerrilla, Gu boiled water and made soup, listening anxiously to the groans from the bedroom. For some reason he felt exhilarated, clear-headed. Buoyed up with confidence he longed for this birth. His face with its stubbly beard glowed red in the firelight. He felt he had been assigned a most important mission, a rather mysterious one, yet could not account for his exuberance.

After Yuyin had finished a big bowl of egg soup, her pains seemed to ease off a little. A strange, somewhat sheepish smile appeared on her face. The maternal pride of a woman about to bring a new life into the world makes her utterly fearless, able to keep death at bay. Leaning back with her legs stretched out, she indicated her rounded womb and said, "This little creature kicking and punching me is a real imp — most likely a bouncing boy! Doesn't care if he kills his mum. . . ."

"Congratulations, Yuyin. Old Man Heaven will bring you through safely, mother and son. . . ." Old Gu, a veteran soldier, was actually talking like someone superstitious.

"With you here . . . I'm not afraid. If not for your coming this evening, I'd have died in agony and nobody would have known." With that her eyes closed and she fell asleep. Perhaps after her pains all day the child in her womb was exhausted too. Or perhaps this was a lull before even worse pains.

Now Gu Yanshan grew frantic. He had been listening for traffic outside. Once Yuyin fell asleep he left the inn and trudged through the wind and snow to wait by the highway. He would stop any vehicle that came along, even if he had to lie down to block the way. The snow stopped presently and the wind died down. The white snow all around lit up the darkness. His hands stuffed in the pockets of his old army coat, he paced up and down anxiously . . . as if on sentry duty. Yes, he had worn this same army coat in the Beiping-Tianjin Campaign, standing in the snow waiting for the signal to launch an all-out offensive and longing for the dawn of victory. . . . How time had flown, and what great changes he'd seen! A man's life is sometimes a riddle even to himself. Over twenty years before, he had stood in the snow on the north China plain ready to shed his blood to usher in a new society. Now he was standing on the snowy highway of a small mountain town in the south, waiting for a truck to give a lift to a woman about to have a child. But what kind of child? The child of two members of the Five Categories, of a couple living in sin, whose very birth was a crime. . . . Life was too complex, too rich for him to fathom. From time to time he looked back at the old inn. How he longed to hear the rumble of a truck and see its powerful headlights sweep over the snow. He had cursed trucks before for scattering dust and mud; but now he thought of them as a means to save Yuyin and her child and rescue him from his dilemma.

At last he was able to flag an army truck on its way to a big army depot near by. When the PLA driver heard what this local cadre with a northern accent wanted, he told him to get in and backed to the end of Old Street.

By the time Old Gu helped Yuyin into the driver's cabin, her pains had started again and she kept groaning. The driver drove fast but steadily straight to the army hospital in a valley.

At once Yuyin was carried to the consulting room on the second floor. The long quiet corridor was brightly lit. Doctors and nurses in white coats shuttled in and out of its glass door, as if her condition were very critical. Old Gu waited by the door, not stirring a step. To him, the consulting room seemed a palace in fairyland, with doctors and nurses in it as immortals, but from which he was debarred as a mere mortal. Before long a doctor with red army insignia visible beneath a white collar brought him a form to fill up. Only when this doctor took off her mask did he see that she was a young woman.

"Are you the patient's husband? What name? What unit?"

Old Gu's cheeks burned. In a fluster he just nodded. What else could he do? It was saving Yuyin that mattered. He stammered out his name and unit. The doctor wrote them down, then told him, "Your wife's no longer young. She has been undernourished and the foetal position's wrong, so she'll have to have a Caesarean. Please sign."

"A Caesarean?" Old Gu stared in dismay. He was

red with embarrassment, but never mind. His heart palpitating he stared for a while at the doctor before getting a grip on himself. He had served in the PLA. It had always loved the people and been responsible to them. In spite of the changes in the last twenty years, he knew that in this respect their attitude hadn't changed. With another nod he took the pen from her and scrawled "Gu Yanshan". Never mind this misunderstanding. For the time being he would take the responsibility of a husband and father.

Yuyin was wheeled out on a stretcher. In the corridor she gripped his hand tightly as he accompanied her to the operating-theatre. As soon as the doctors and nurses had gone in, the door was closed. Again he waited outside, pacing up and down, burning with anxiety. He listened eagerly for the infant's first cry. Yuyin must have lost so much blood. . . . How great life was, how wonderful to be a mother, giving birth to a new life. It was people that filled the world with joy and grief. Why should there be grief and hatred? Especially in our Party, in the society the workers and peasants had fought for and of which they were the masters? Why have these endless struggles year after year? Some bloodthirsty carecrists made it their job to do others down. Why? He couldn't understand this. He hadn't much education, didn't know what was meant by the "theory of human nature". His level was too low. Yet he had been poisoned by it and the theory of the dying out of class struggle. . . .

Four hours dragged by filled with these bitter reflections. At dawn Yuyin was wheeled out. Beside her lay a little creature in snowy white swaddling-clothes. But her face was as white as paper, her eyes were closed. "Is she dead?" Old Gu blurted out, his eyes filling with tears. The nurse wheeling Yuyin noticed his despair. "All's well," she said. "The mother hasn't come to yet after the anaesthetic. . . ." "So she's come through!" he exclaimed, forgetting even to ask the sex of the baby. "She's come through!" This cry re-echoed through the quiet corridor of the hospital.

It was the hospital's rule that mothers and infants must be separated. A paper slip marked with a number was attached to the baby's swaddling-clothes. Gu Yanshan was allowed into the ward where Yuyin was being given an intravenous drip. Not until noon did she come to. At once her eyes fell on Old Gu. She reached out a feeble hand and laid it in his. Like a fond, overjoyed husband he was stroking her hand when a nurse came in to tell the "couple" that their baby was a plump, vociferous boy. His number was 7011. This news reduced Yuyin to tears, and Old Gu's eyes reddened too. To the nurse this was nothing unusual: when middle-aged couples had their first child they always wept for joy. She gave Yuyin an injection to make her sleep, and asked, "What name are you going to give your son?"

Yuyin glanced at Old Gu, but without consulting him said, "Gu Jun — the *jun* for army." Then she dozed off.

To give her time to recuperate, and because the roads were drifted over with snow, Old Gu made Yuyin stay in hospital for more than fifty days. He went there from Hibiscus every morning and stayed until the evening. Luckily he was only a nominal adviser in the grain depot with no real responsibilities. Soon the whole township heard that the new rich peasant Hu Yuyin had a plump boy fathered by Qin Shutian, now in a labour camp. But this news left them cold. Still, after her return to the inn some kind-hearted old ladies went secretly to have a look at her ill-starred boy, and left her some boiled eggs.

Gu Yanshan was summoned to the grain bureau and security bureau in the county to account for what had happened. But both the grain commissioner and the head of the security bureau had come south with the army with him and were well-disposed to their old comrade-in-arms. They knew he was a decent sort, not likely to shine but incapable of doing anything really wrong. Besides, being impotent he couldn't have it off with a woman; so after cracking some jokes at his expense they let the matter drop. And when later more material on Old Gu was sent in by the revolutionary committees of Hibiscus and the commune, it was ignored. Even Secretary Yang Min'gao simply scoffed, "This is piddling, not worth reporting." However, Old Gu was penalized by not being allowed to attend his Party branch meetings.

And so Old Gu was acknowleged to have the right to care for Yuyin and her son. Right up to the fall of the "gang of four", by which time the boy was seven or eight, Old Gu and Yuyin took good care of each other although not even related. Old Gu said, "Soon Qin Shutian will be back, we must give the boy another surname Qin." Anyway the child was "black", not recognized by the commune or the brigade or given a residence card. Gu Yanshan was "foster-father" to this little "black devil". This was one of the wonders of Hibiscus in the later stage of the "cultural revolution".

"Dad," said Yuyin one day, addressing Old Gu as

her son did. "There's talk in town that folk have sent in a petition asking to have you made secretary and chairman of Hibiscus. And the higher-ups have approved. Wang Qiushe will have to scuttle back to that rickety stilt-house of his! In fact, in our new society with a people's government, it's old cadres like you who ought to be in charge."

"Don't you believe it, Yuyin." Old Gu shook his head with a wry smile. "I'm still not allowed to attend Party meetings. I'll be left dangling like this, unless Li Guoxiang and Yang Min'gao are dismissed or transferred."

"We're to blame, dad, sonny and I. . . . All these years you've been under a cloud because of us. . . ." Yuyin burst into tears.

"My, your eyes are like springs never running dry," he scolded affectionately. Caressing the boy he went on reassuringly, "There's been a change for the better. Instructions have come from above that you and Shutian must be cleared. If they really were to put me in charge of Hibiscus, I wouldn't be able to cope. The place is a shambles. We'd have to start from scratch. First of all we'd have to deal with the problem of water contamination in Hibiscus. Keeps me awake at night . . . ."

Before taking up his post the "soldier from the north" had insomnia. Yuyin smiled through her tears. Her small son laughed, then exclaimed:

"Mum! Dad! They say Uncle Mangeng's to be secretary of the brigade again. Yesterday evening he promised to give me a residence card — I won't be black any more!"

# The Collapse of the Stilt-House

Life often plays cruel tricks on people who break faith.

These years shame and remorse had flayed Li Mangeng like an invisible yet ruthless whip. He had a guilty conscience because he had sold out the love of his youth, gone back on his word. When Hu Yuyin was proclaimed a new rich peasant and Li Guigui killed himself, he had joined in denouncing them. In his distraction he sometimes raised his hands to sniff at them, as if they still reeked of blood.

But Mangeng's life was a blend of loyalty and betrayal. He had betrayed his sister Yuyin whom he had truly loved, broken the promise he made to her by the river. Yet when he gave the work team from the county the one thousand five hundred yuan she had left in his keeping, that showed his loyalty to the Party. What a complex contradiction! Back in 1956, when working in the district government, to prove his loyalty to the Party he had sacrificed his love. For when it came to choosing between the Party and an individual, the revolution and love, his reason always triumphed over his emotions. He obeyed the Party implicitly, quite blindly, without any doubts whatsoever or any attempts to analyse its line. His level was too low for that. Obedience was second nature to him. True, he knew of many higher-ups with bad class origins and complex social connections who had succeeded in the war years in combining revolution with love and reason with emotion — some had even married on the execution ground. Working for the same cause had determined what they loved and hated. But that was during the war when blood had to be shed; so of course they had to enlarge their ranks, and anybody could join — the door was wide open. . . . Now the country was theirs to hold on to. The ranks had to be purified. The revolution needed incessant struggles and purges inside the Party. To ensure that a man was sound, his forbears and family must be investigated. And so a revolutionary might have to give up the girl he loved and act against his conscience. What was this invisible conscience anyway? Only the petty-bourgeoisie set store by it. . . . So Mangeng had sold out Yuyin, shoved her into a fiery pit.

But now history had drawn a conclusion, had proved that Yuyin should not have been classified as a rich peasant, or Li Guigui hounded to death. You contemptible informer, Li Mangeng, you selfish swine, you stooge whose hands reek of blood, do you count as a Communist? Are you up to being a real Communist? Which Party rule or directive told you to do such things? You can't blame it on other people. There are thirty-eight million Party members in China, but few have sold out their own sisters or supported tyranny. Who can you blame, you brute?

Mangeng often swore at himself like this. But was he entirely to blame? Was he born a wicked bully? Had he never done anything good for Yuyin and the townsfolk? Never been sincere and honest? Apparently not. Ah, Hu Yuyin the old innkeeper's darling daughter had been the bane of his life. Even when she was paraded in the streets with a black placard as a rich peasant widow, made to go up on the stage to be struggled against, he had never treated her roughly or jeered at her. . . . For that he had been criticized many times by the brigade Party branch and the revolutionary committee of the town. They denounced his Rightist tendency, his denial of the class character of human nature, his failure to take an active part in class struggle. He was dismissed from his post as secretary, all but expelled from the Party. What was the class character of human nature? He had only been to primary school, hadn't much of a brain, and very little imagination. This theory of human nature stuck in his throat like a hunk of chaff and wild herbs which he couldn't chew up, swallow or spit out — it might give him throat cancer. Wretched and unable to describe his frustration, he was detested both by Yuyin and the Party. Like the soil squeezed into a crack in the rocks, all he asked for was to survive. You didn't know where you were with all these movements and struggles. You tried to keep in step with them, to be loyal, but they kept you dangling like a performing monkey. . . .

"You worm, Li Mangeng! You worm!" For years he had suffered from depression. A big brawny fellow able to carry a hundred pounds and walk a hundred *li*, his broad shoulders now stooped as if under a great load. Finally even his wife Peppery was afraid that he was ill.

Peppery herself was a complex character. When Yuyin did so well with her beancurd stall and Peppery suspected her husband of still hankering after her, jealously kept her scolding like a shrew. She later made a great scene over that one thousand five hundred yuan, sobbing and screaming till Mangeng was forced to hand it in. She had even gloated over Yuyin's misfortune, which increased her own sense of security. Now her husband should lose interest in the Hibiscus Fairy.

But as time went by and Yuyin was paraded year after year with that black placard, Peppery felt this was wrong. No woman, however bad, should be victimized all her life. . . . Her husband pulled a long face the whole time, but she knew without being told what was on his mind. She sometimes felt guilty herself. When Yuyin had a baby, she went to the inn like a thief in the night for a look. He was a plump bonny baby, his hands and feet as pudgy as lotus roots. Was he a bastard? No, people called him Junjun and his father was the Rightist Qin Shutian, now doing time in a labour camp.

When Junjun was big enough to romp, Peppery would call him into their house to give him a sweet. The little scamp had more than his share of good looks, with big bright eyes like his parents. Peppery had a weakness for him, because her last two children had been two more girls — she had six daughters now. And gradually she noticed that Mangeng had a soft spot for Junjun too. He smiled whenever the boy came in, took to hugging him and making much of him. Well, she was glad to see him in a good mood. If he went on moping all the time he would really go into a decline; then she and her six daughters would have to beg for their living!

"Here, Junjun, have some fruit." Sometimes when Mangeng had goodies for his daughters he kept a share for Junjun.

"No, mum would scold me. She says if I eat in other people's homes they'll look down on us." The boy rattled this off without reaching out for the fruit, though he had fixed his eyes on it longingly. Already he had begun to be torn between his feelings and reason. Peppery, watching him, took pity on the boy.

"Junjun," she said, "you and your mum have only

one grain ration between you. Do you get enough to eat?"

"Mum always makes me eat first. Then eats what's left. If I won't eat she spanks me, then hugs me and cries. . . ." His eyes turned red. So did those of Mangeng and Peppery. They knew how hard it must be for a widow forced to sweep the streets every day under supervision to bring up a growing boy on one grain ration. They themselves had been much better off since Mangeng stopped being a cadre. A good farmer, he earned many workpoints in the brigade and grew enough vegetables on their own plot to feed their family of eight and sell the surplus every market-day. Peppery and the girls had done so well raising pigs and poultry, they made a lot of money. Husband and wife had won through hardships to share better days. Now that they were older and had so many children, she had got over her jealousy and they had achieved domestic harmony.

After the fall of the "gang of four", in retrospect people had gained a better understanding of themselves — something no money can buy. Each had kept tabs on all those years of political movements and struggles. Now some corrected their mistakes, repented of their crimes. Those with nothing on their conscience could sleep in peace. Those who had been too vicious could not escape retribution.

Mangeng and Peppery often kept Junjun to a meal or to play with their girls.

"Junjun, does your mum know where you're eating?"

"Yes."

"Has she scolded you?"

"No, just called me a little beggar. . . ."

Apparently Yuyin gave her tacit consent. Once Peppery called in a tailor to make New Year clothes for her six girls, and a suit for Junjun too. When this was ready she wrapped it up in paper and told him to take it home to show his mum. Very soon he was back, dressed in his brand-new suit, to show Mangeng and Peppery.

"Did your mum tell you to wear it?"

"Yes. And to come and thank uncle and aunt."

At the start of spring the ice melted. Spring thunder rumbled earlier than usual and rain came pouring down. One afternoon Li Mangeng and Wang Qiushe were summoned to an enlarged meeting of the commune Party committee convened by the commune and municipality. The new Party secretary of the commune gave the stilt-house owner a sharp reprimand for failing to rehabilitate Hu Yuyin and Qin Shutian, and for not returning her new house and one thousand five hundred yuan. On behalf of the county committee he removed Wang from his posts as Party secretary of the brigade and chairman of the Hibiscus revolutionary committee. The brigade was to come under the leadership of the town's revolutionary committee, and for the time being, pending an election, its Party branch would be headed by its former secretary Li Mangeng. The county would appoint a new head for the Hibiscus Party committee and revolutionary committee. Wang Qiushe scuttled away in consternation before this appointment was announced, forgetting to take his cape and hat but rushing off bare-headed through the rain. For a while the clapping and cheering at the meeting drowned out the sound of the pelting rain and thunder.

The meeting did not break up till the evening. It was

ten *li* to Mangeng's home and, in spite of wearing a bamboo hat, by the time he got there he was drenched to the skin. But he felt warm, exhilarated though rather chastened. He had been reinstated as secretary and Wang Qiushe's dismissal had rid the town of a pest. The townsfolk in their jubilation might even let off fire-crackers to send off his ghost.

"So you've got your old job back?" Peppery demanded as she watched him change his clothes. "You've picked up that rotten official cap other people would chuck away, and stuck it on your head, eh?"

"How did you hear so quickly?"

"When you went with the Autumn Snake to that meeting, it was the talk of the town. People came to ask me the reason, but what did *I* know? Well, it's no business of mine, so long as you sow our private plot and chop firewood. If you don't we won't let you into the house. Don't think you can loaf about here the way you used to."

"All right, whatever you say. Don't worry, I have a yen now for tilling our private plot. . . . Besides, a piddling little official like me has to take part in production. The higher-ups have told us to fix farm output quotas for each team, in some cases for each household, so no one can slack."

"Did you know that Wang Qiushe, that lazy snake, came rushing back in the rain, ranting and raving?"

"Raving about what?"

"He kept screeching, 'They've let the big shots go, but nabbed the small fry!' and 'Never forget class struggle. . . . There'll be new cultural revolutions every five or six years!' Well, he's got what was coming to him — it's driven him round the bend!"

"No wonder. When output quotas are fixed, which team will want him? Give him a few fields, he'd only grow weeds on them. . . . He can't go on living off being an activist!"

As they were talking, over the roar of the storm outside their window they heard a deafening crash.

"Whose house is that?" Mangeng shuddered. Peppery turned white. Most of the wooden houses on the old flagstone street had not been repaired for years. Which of them had collapsed?

Mangeng roled up his trouser legs, put on his coir cape and bamboo hat and was preparing to go out when they heard a yell from the street. It sounded like the announcement of good news:

"It's the stilt-house! The stilt-house has collapsed . . . ."

## "He Will Love Her All His Life"

Hu Yuyin swept the flagstone street alone first thing each morning. For how many years now? She swept away in silence, never pausing to look up. What was she thinking? Of the way Qin Shutian had wielded his broom as if rowing a boat on stage? Of the trick they had played on Li Guoxiang and Wang Qiushe when they lorded it over Hibiscus? Was she looking for Qin's footprints, which had made each flagstone shine? She could not tell his footprints from her own, but they were engraved on the flagstones and on her heart. She drew strength from her memories of the man she loved. Strange, in all these years, shamefully treated as a class enemy and hard put to it to survive, she had never thought of committing suicide. She had learned from Qin how to cope. When summoned to a struggle meeting, she went as calmly as if setting out to work, hung her head before others could yank it down, knelt before they could kick her from behind. . . . All these struggles had turned her into another "old campaigner", deserving a gold medal. In all those years of ultra-Left contests, why were no gold, silver or bronze medals issued?

This way she got off more lightly. At each struggle meeting she knelt motionless facing the townsfolk with no expression on her face as pale as alabaster. Sometimes she raised her big bright eyes to look sadly at the crowd. Was she hoping to arouse their sympathy, to undermine their fighting spirit? Was this a silent protest: "Look, neighbours, I'm Sister Hibiscus who once sold beancurd. I'll kneel to you until you take pity on me and let me go. . . ." Indeed, each time she knelt on the stage during a struggle meeting, the atmosphere was less militant than usual, smelt less strongly of gunpowder. Some people hung their heads unwilling to watch, or the rims of their eyes reddened. Others made an excuse to leave early, though there were militiamen on guard at the doors.

The birds in the trees, the plants in a ditch all have their own fate. And so did Hu Yuyin. Everything in life is fated. Otherwise with so many women lazier, more spiteful or more vicious than she was, why had she got into such trouble for working so hard from dawn till dark to sell beancurd? What good were those people who asked for relief every year? Yet the authorities thought highly of them. The magistrates in the old days had despised the poor and pandered to the rich; but now they had gone to the other extreme, victimizing the rich and pandering to the poor, without asking how they had made or lost their money. And a fellow like Wang Qiushe was considered an activist. Well, Yuyin, you've made a fine mess of this life; in your next you'd better be a greedy slacker and hold out your hand for relief. Follow the example of Wang Qiushe, who propped up his rickety stilt-house with wooden buttresses and held on to his poor-peasant status to please higher-ups and be petted by them as an activist in every movement.

Well, she had no intention of dying, she would live on shamelessly even though they treated her like a black-hearted devil. She had a true love now, Brother Shutian still in the labour camp, and he had left her their precious little Junjun. So she wouldn't die. Life was worth living no matter how hard. She had raised the boy with kisses and caresses, and now he was eight years old. His dad had been sentenced to ten years' hard labour. Now nine had gone, so he should soon be back. He had written her every month from the labour camp by Dongting Lake, ending each letter with "kisses for little Junjun". Were they only for Junjun? She knew what her husband meant. . . . She wrote to him every month, "Junjun sends you a kiss. Look after your health and remould yourself well so that you'll be let out earlier. We long for you every day. I've nearly worn my eyes out watching for you. But don't worry, Junjun's growing bigger each year and I'm not all that old. My heart's still young, I've kept it young for you. Don't worry, you mustn't worry."

Yes, she still remembered the hundred-odd songs of *Wedding Songs*, could still sing them all. She and Qin would sing them together when he was released. Did you tell him that in your letters, Yuyin? Don't be afraid, those songs are no secret code, they're just against feudalism, so the warder should give him your letters.

Yuyin was up at dawn every day to sweep the street in silence. She wasn't just sweeping but searching for their footprints on the flagstones.... Two years after the fall of the "gang of four" she was notified by the brigade: "Hu Yuyin, you needn't sweep the street any more." But she went on just the same. For one thing she was afraid they might change their minds and accuse her of reversing the verdict against her; for another, she was used to it and wanted to show the townsfolk that she meant to go on until her husband's return. She said nothing, but her heart was brimming with love.

In the spring of 1979, the town's revolutionary committee sent a man, who had denounced her and notified her that she was a new rich peasant, to announce: "You were classified wrongly, now we're changing back your status to that of a small trader. The property rights of the new house are yours again, but we want to borrow it for the time being."

Yuyin covered her eyes in fright, unable to believe this. Impossible! It must be a dream.... Tears trickled through her fingers, but she held back her sobs. She was afraid to uncover her eyes and find that it was a dream. Impossible.... After being a rich peasant for fifteen years, struggled against so often and forced to kneel, to put up with endless hardships — how could they just say "you were classified wrongly"? Besides, they liked playing tricks, and he was one of those who had made her a rich peasant. They were capable of anything. How could they be wrong? So Yuyin did not believe it.

She did not believe it till she was shown the directive from the county government, with the bright red seal of the Public Security Bureau. Heavens! She very nearly fainted away. She staggered but did not fall. Those hard years had toughened her. Her face suddenly flushed crimson. Widening her eyes she held out her arms and cried in a ringing voice which even startled herself:

"I'm in no hurry for the house or that money. First give me back my man! It's my husband I want!"

The cadres of the town's revolutionary committee were astounded. They thought this woman so silent all these years was asking them for Li Guigui who had killed himself in 1964! They blenched. What a woman! Just cleared, her cap removed, instead of kowtowing her thanks she made such an unreasonable demand!

Her arms still outstretched, Yuyin went on more quietly, "Give me back my husband. . . . You put him in prison, sentenced him to ten years — he's only got one more to go. He's not guilty of any crimes. . . ."

At that they sighed with relief and told her with smiles, "Qin Shutian has been cleared too. It was wrong to make him a Rightist. He's to get back his old job. Two evenings ago the provincial radio station broadcast his *Wedding Songs*."

Yuyin laughed hysterically. "So it was all wrong! Brother Shutian's case too! What a joke! Heavens, we're back in the new society! The Communist Party's come back — its policies too. . . ."

Yuyin in all her forty years had never made such a scene in the street, never laughed so wildly or uncontrollably. She danced for joy, her hair tumbling over her shoulders. Thinking she had gone mad, the townsfolk pitied her. When her small son came to tug at her sleeve she picked him up, whirled him round and kissed his cheeks before taking him back to the inn.

Once home she threw herself on the bed and sobbed. Why? One should cry for despair not for joy! Human beings are strange creatures, for they shed tears to vent both grief and joy.

The next day, bright and early, Yuyin took her bamboo broom to sweep the street. Hitherto she had done this in subdued silence, but today she was in high spirits. Now that she was cleared there was no need for her to go on with this sweeping, but she wanted in this way to express her thanks to the townsfolk for not hounding her to death but leaving her a way out. She hadn't come to grief because of them, but because of the policy decided above. And now that her luck had changed, what was shameful about going on sweeping the street? The people who should feel ashamed were the ones who in the new society begged for food, for relief, for subsidies. She had heard that in big cities like Beijing and Shanghai street-sweepers were called sanitation workers, and some of them were people's deputies whose photographs appeared in the newspapers.

In fact, Yuyin had another secret reason for getting up so early to sweep the street. She knew that as soon as Qin was notified that he had been cleared, he would hurry back day and night as fast as he could. He had never seen his son, and must wonder how much his wife had aged in nine years. She knew how frantic he must have been feeling. At night she couldn't sleep. But

little Junjun slept so soundly that even when she hugged
him he didn't wake. Night after night she listened in
vain for footsteps, for knocking at the gate. She had a
hunch that Qin would come back in the morning. She
had heard that the bus from the district to the county
arrived in the afternoon. It was sixty *li* from the county
to Hibiscus, and rather than spend a night in town he'd
walk along the highway. Yes, walk all night. . . .

By the time the street was swept the sun was up, but
still no sign of him. She thought resentfully: Men are
so thoughtless. If you can't leave because of some red
tape, you should at least write me a letter or send me
a wire. I've cricked my neck looking out for you, you
wretch! Can you be waiting in the county town to get
back your old job? Pah, men set too much store by their
careers. She didn't want him to go back to that job
which could so easily land him in trouble. Just stay
here with Yuyin and look after Junjun. We can till our
private plot, raise pigs and poultry and work in the
brigade; spruce up our storeyed house and live in
comfort. . . .

These years of victimization had left Yuyin rather
fearful and suspicious. She was afraid of another change
in line and fresh cries of "Down with the new rich peasant!" Militiamen might suddenly hang a black placard
on her again, hustle her off to a struggle meeting and
force her to kneel. She lived in fear and trembling,
hardly able to wait for Brother Shutian to come back.
Even if these good times lasted a few days only, they
could hold up their heads and walk side by side in the
street like other couples, laughing and chatting together.
Do hurry up and come back, what's keeping you,

brother? If they put those labels on us again before we meet, we can't fight against fate. . . .

This morning was misty with hoarfrost, rather chilly when she went to sweep the street. She felt limp, not having slept well. She had grown tired of watching for her husband. She cried with disappointment every night, and had to change her pillow-case the next morning. If he didn't come back, how could she count as cleared? Life was so futile without him. She felt tempted to go and make a scene, to ask the town's revolutionary committee: Why is my husband still not back? Why haven't you carried out the policy? . . . She swished her broom over the flagstones, stopping at the corner of the co-op wall to lean against it and rest. Instinctively she peered round at the side gate where Wang Qiushe had come a cropper that year. It was now blocked up with bricks. Who cares! Why think about the past. . . .

As she took up her broom again, she saw a figure with a hold-all striding towards her. He must be hurrying to catch the first bus. Well, he should have asked the way. The bus station was in the opposite direction. Still he came striding towards her. She'd wait till he came closer, then direct him. . . . Her broom swished over the flagstones. . . .

"Yuyin? Yuyin, Yuyin!"

Who was calling her so early? She couldn't see too clearly. A tall, lean bearded fellow in new clothes was standing in front of her. He had put down his hold-all and stood stock-still . . . Yuyin fell back a step.

"Yuyin, Yuyin!" he cried, then held out his arms.

To her annoyance she could not make out who he was. She felt dazed. Was he Brother Shutian? Or was she dreaming again? Was he her husband for whom she had been longing? Surely not. How could he appear so easily out of the blue? She trembled, nearly choking. Then at the top of her voice she cried:

"Brother Shutian!"

Qin threw his strong arms around her, hugging her tight and lifting her off the ground. Yuyin clung to him like a vine, her eyes closed, her face white as carved jade. She let him hug her, pricking her cheeks with his beard, conscious only that her man was back. It wasn't a dream, he was really and truly back.

The broom had fallen across the flagstone street. Qin carried Yuyin to the co-op steps to sit down, holding her close to him.

"Brother Shutian! You, you. . . ." she sobbed.

"Don't cry, Yuyin! Don't cry. . . ."

"You didn't write to tell me. Day and night I've been waiting. . . . I knew you'd hurry back."

"What time did I have to write? I was busy catching a steamer, a train, a bus, and then I walked all night, cursing myself for not having wings. I covered a thousand *li* in only three days. Are you still not happy, Yuyin?"

"It's for you I've kept living, brother."

"That goes for me too. If not for you, I'd have drowned myself in Dongting Lake."

Yuyin suddenly stopped crying, threw her arms around his neck and covered his face with kisses.

"My beard's too long, I didn't stop to shave it."

"How does a man know what's in a woman's heart?"

"I know your heart."

"Each morning sweeping the street I called your name and spoke to you — did you know that?"

"I knew. Each morning cutting reeds or dredging mud from the lake, I answered you. I knew you were sweeping the street, starting up at that end and stopping here to rest. I could hear the swish of your broom."

"Hold me! Hold me tight! I'm cold."

She nestled up to him as if afraid he might suddenly let go of her and vanish.

"Yuyin, Yuyin ... what a hard life you've had, love...." It was Qin's turn to cry. "You've been through hell because of me.... I shall never be able to make it up to you. All these years my one wish was to come back to see you once more.... I never dreamed Old Man Heaven would open his eyes and let us start living as human beings again...."

Yuyin stroked his unkempt hair and said soothingly, "I'm not crying, brother, so why should you? 'He will love her all his life.' I remember mum telling me: Someone who's loved can win through any hardships.... That's what I've felt all these years — we've come together again. Let's get up now. If early risers see us sitting on the co-op steps like this, how they'll laugh!"

Qin was still shedding tears as they stood up. Like a young couple head over heels in love they went back arm-in-arm to the inn.

"Junjun's eight now, isn't he? Will he call me dad?"

"I taught him to long ago. Every day he asks when his dad will be back, he can hardly wait.... But listen to me, I won't have it if you dote on the boy and leave me out in the cold."

"What nonsense you do talk!"

# The Knell of an Age

This spring saw a great change in the Hibiscus market. In the past when folk from the hills had gone there to peddle furs, herbs and other mountain products, they had to have eyes in the back of their heads to see which way the wind was blowing. It was forbidden to sell grain, tea oil, peanuts, soya beans, cotton, timber, pigs, cows and goats, of which the state had the monopoly. As for pork and beef, they rarely tasted these from one end of the year to the other, being forced to sell even their suckling-pigs. The townsfolk's meat ration was half a pound per head a month, sometimes only obtainable through the back door. Oddly enough this shortage was used by the press to publicize modern medicine. Animal fat had a high cholesterol content, conducive to hardening of the arteries, high blood pressure and heart disease; thus many countries had cut down their meat consumption to eat more coarse grains and vegetables, the cellulose of which was good for the health. Someone plump and ruddy might suddenly drop dead; being lean could lengthen your life.

What amazing tricks time played! Little over two years after the fall of the "gang" a completely new age started for the townsfolk. Now Hibiscus had a market six times a month. To it flocked gaily dressed Yao and Zhuang girls with sparkling silver trinkets, smartly turned out Han youngsters, housewives and householders with bulging purses, beaming with satisfaction. Some came in couples or small groups, carrying loads of lush shallots or crisp, fresh cabbages, cratefuls or basketfuls of speckled eggs and pale green ducks' eggs, or pushing barrows loaded with live fish. Some cycled there with a smiling girl on their carrier. . . . They came streaming in from all sides by highways and byways, and set up their stalls along New Street and Old Street. The little town rang with their voices. . . .

Today what aroused most attention were a new rice market and a meat market. White rice, red rice, coarse rice, polished rice — you could take your pick then haggle over the price. For the new policy allowed commune members who had sold their quota to the state to sell their surplus products in this market. The meat market was an impressive sight, like a display of home-raised pigs where you looked for the biggest sides, the thinnest skin and the most succulent pork.

"Reckon that pig weighs about three hundred pounds, eh?"

"Three hundred! Not worth fattening any more."

"Ha, it's run to fat, too little lean, the wife dislikes too much grease. . . ."

"No pleasing you, is there, comrade? Think back two years to that half a pound ration a month, when you'd no oil to fry your vegetables. Now you don't like fat, want more lean!"

Yes, the times had certainly changed. Even on days when there was no market, the butchers in Old Street and New Street sold pork from morning to night. A new contradiction cropped up in the co-op: the commune members delivered more pigs than they could take. The town was too small to have a refrigeration plant, the commune members couldn't get rid of their pigs, and how could the state sell so many? The supply exceeded the demand — a far cry from the old days. The townsfolk did not know what exactly was meant by the "four modernizations", but already they were having a taste of their advantages.

They also had cause for concern. With memories of the past fresh in their minds, some of them wondered uneasily if the ultra-Left line would make a sudden come-back and stamp out these hopeful new developments. Would their lives be filled again with slogans, theories, struggles and political movements instead of oil, salt, fuel and rice for their daily needs. . . . This seemed a real possibility. Since Wang Qiushe went mad he had slouched through New Street and Old Street every day, bright golden Chairman Mao badges on his ragged tunic, howling like a banshee:

"Never forget class struggle!"

"Every five or six years we'll have a new cultural revolution."

His eerie shrieks could be heard all over Hibiscus. In the daytime when the townsfolk saw him coming, they ran indoors and shut their gates. After dark his howls made their hair stand on end. Yuyin, now an attendant in the beancurd shop on Old Street, would spill a bowl of soup at the sound. In the homes of the tax-officer and head of the co-op, just reinstated, these yells made the grown-ups shed tears, the children cry. It was hard to sleep at night. The stilt-house owner was still plaguing Hibiscus.

The apprehensive townsfolk swore at him.

As Sister Hibiscus fondled her little son's head she worried, "Crazy Wang isn't going to starve or freeze to death, how many years will he live?"

Li Mangeng's wife Peppery demanded, "Does that crazy Wang, stark bonkers, expect to be mayor or secretary again, forcing us to recite quotations and dance the loyalty dance?"

Her husband, brigade Party secretary, told her, "Never mind that lunatic! In our new society led by the Party, hoodlums like Wang Qiushe won't get anywhere. We've learned a bitter lesson."

Gu Yanshan the "soldier from the north", now secretary of the town committee, was too busy cleaning up Hibiscus River and Jade-leaf Stream to express any opinion. Instead he decided to have Wang sent to the district's mental hospital for treatment — sending off the God of Plague.

Qin Shutian, the deputy head of the county's cultural centre, had recently come back to Hibiscus to collect folk-songs. His comment showed the wide range of his experience and understanding. "Nowadays aren't there raving lunatics wandering through most cities and towns? They're sounding the knell of a terrible, tragic age."

# Postscript

I was born in 1942 in the northern foothills of the Wuling Mountains in south Hunan. That small village had no more than fifty households who lived north and south of some narrow fields, like two elephants standing side by side, and so the place was called Two Elephants Village. The west end was screened by a fine stand of cypresses, deep green the whole year round. A winding flagstone road ran from north to south, while from east to west flowed a brook called "Bigger than a Ditch". For us kids, in summer and autumn that brook was our "Happy River". Stark naked we learned to dive and swim dog-paddle. We had water fights and caught snails, fish, shrimps, crabs and eels, our small hands reaching boldly into the cracks of the rocks, from which occasionally we might pull out a slippery bream. We stirred up the green water till it was muddy. But it was starting with that little brook that some boys of my age later joined our glorious navy and sailed the high seas. And, even more unpredictably, one of those bare-bottomed boys took to writing stories.

Behind that little village was a big primeval forest, lush and green. In the daytime of course that was our favourite playground where we gathered firewood, pine needles, mushrooms and bamboo shoots and learned to shin up trees like squirrels to raid birds' nests. After dark we found it a scary, spooky place. The sound of wind and rain, the soughing of pines and the cries of birds and beasts frightened us into tucking our heads inside our quilts and gave us nightmares. When I woke with a start from dreams of falling out of a window, off a roof, off the top of a tree or down from the sky, the grown-ups said I was outgrowing my strength.

Climbing trees I grazed my hands and feet and tore my clothes, for which I often had my bottom spanked, my head rapped with a bamboo. Those tall tree tops which brushed the clouds and seemed to soar to the moon and stars had a great attraction for me. But actually I never once climbed to the top. The grown-ups had warned me that coiled in the crows' nests up there lay speckled snakes. The thought of that made me look down. But it's no good looking down when you're climbing a tree. It made me so dizzy, my hands and feet so limp that I quickly slithered down, ignoring the squirrels mocking me from the boughs. . . . Later, when I started writing, I often remembered those climbs of mine as a boy, the attraction they had for me and the spice of danger. It was really difficult to climb to the top.

In those days that small village near the border was culturally very backward. Only a few times a year did travelling showmen come from Henan or Anhui with their performing monkeys, and of course there were none of the broadcasts, films or modern plays that villages have today. But that mountain village had its own old culture. My home was known in Hunan for its folk-songs, and the women sang and danced whenever there was a wedding. Each time a village girl married, all the other girls and young wives came to sing in her home for three days to give her a send-off. They sang about her reluctance to leave her childhood home, her hopes for her marriage, her parents' grief at this parting. An even more common theme was aversion to feudal conventions and arranged marriages. (After Liberation musicians came to our parts to study the local customs, and they recorded six to seven hundred of these traditional songs.) Every autumn, when the grain was in the barns and the sickles hung on the walls, was the season for weddings at which such songs were sung. We kids were always able to tuck in by reaching out a row of small hands for titbits. We were able to feast our eyes on the decorated bridal sedan chair as it was borne into the village, and the bride in her red silk veil as she and the bridegroom bowed together to Heaven and Earth then went into the bridal chamber. We could also give our ears treat by standing quietly behind the singers while they sang:

> A bride of eighteen, a groom of three
> Who wet the bed each night,
> Less than a pillow in length,
> Not up to a broom in height.
> At night he woke, for milk he cried.
> "I'm not your mum — I'm your bride!"

Another cultural activity in that small mountain village was listening to stories. Old folk told stories to pass the time and in this way taught the youngsters some culture and history. In those days, in times of peace, there was practically nothing to do in the country at night. People could relax and be quiet — there were no meetings. The only sounds were cocks crowing or dogs barking, or a sudden commotion if a thief was caught trying to steal a water-buffalo. Of course we kids had to work in exchange for listening to stories. In summer we sat on the threshing-ground in the moonlight waving rush fans to cool the old story-teller and drive away mosquitoes; in winter by the brazier we pummelled his back muscles which ached after the day's labours. As time went by my little brain became crammed with *The Canonization of the Gods*, *The Pilgrimage to the West*, *Outlaws of the Marsh* and other old stories.

Perhaps, without my knowing it, the seeds of literature were sown in my childish mind by the brook beside the village, the forest behind it, the wedding songs I heard and the stories the old folk told. Those seeds certainly fell on very poor rocky soil, and could hardly have germinated without the spring wind and rain.

I confess to my shame that the first books I read were stories about swordsmen. Soon after Liberation, when I was eleven or twelve, some dog-eared books with the first and last pages missing circulated through the countryside, most of them the adventures of swordsmen or accounts of involved court cases. I was spellbound by the exploits of those swordsmen who flew on to eaves, climbed high walls and broke into houses to kill scoundrels and save the poor, as well as by all the magic of those immortals and alchemists who rode on clouds and mist and turned stone into gold. Luckily these books did not lead me astray, because most of them were written to the same formula, and by the time the swordsmen reached a dead end the situation could only be saved by the intervention of Guanyin or some other deity.

My tastes were fairly catholic. I read a little of everything: Tang romances, Ming and Qing stories, the new literature of the May 4th period, and the critical realist works of 18th and 19th-century Europe. My favourite novel was *A Dream of Red Mansions*, which I read five or six times, sometimes reading it as a literary textbook, but never understanding it completely. It is truly a great treasury of art. Each time I read some classic it transported me into a colourful world with a whole gallery of characters, so that I felt as if drinking from a crystal fountain. Needless to say my study of great works whether Chinese or foreign was somewhat superficial. Without fully understanding them I tried to adopt their good points in the hope of producing something new myself. Later I also read histories, works on philosophy, war reminiscences, biographies of famous men and records of important world events. I tried to broaden my vision. No one poorly read and ignorant can be a good writer. I thought, since I came from the countryside, if I took no interest in and knew nothing about major current events, simply giving lively factual accounts of a few villagers, it would be hard to avoid mediocrity in my writing.

Literary writing requires nourishment which comes partly from life, partly from reading. If you are widely read in the best works ancient and modern, Chinese and foreign, you are imperceptibly influenced by them. Silently, like rain and dew, they enrich and transform your mind. While trying my hand at writing I often felt that I lacked nourishment. We middle-aged and young writers today have read much less than the older generation of writers.

Just as peasants cultivate their fields, writers cultivate their lives. For life is the soil of literature. Brought up in a poor family in a south Hunan village, when I was only twelve I was faced with the contradiction between getting an education and making a living. Naturally food for my belly had precedence over mental sustenance. First I made straw sandals and sold them, then felled bamboo, carried charcoal to the market and hired myself out as a water-buffalo boy. Our village was so poor that many families took loads of charcoal to other counties to sell. In the sweltering summer the flagstones scorched the soles of your feet, and the sweat pouring off you steamed. On wet days I wrapped straw ropes round my sandals to keep from slipping. In winter the frost chapped my hands and feet so that blood dripped from the raw flesh. But it's the poor who help the poor, and we charcoal pedlars had plenty of homes to stop at to rest and wipe off our sweat — no one would be stranded half-way. If your charcoal or bamboo happened to fetch a good price, you'd buy a few pounds of meat and make a savoury stew with black soya beans, then give your mates a treat. . . . That life taught me how fine it was to earn your own living, taught me how hard this was. It enabled me to appreciate the sterling qualities of the labouring people who share their griefs and joys and help each other out.

Three years later I passed the entrance examination to junior middle school, but still went home in the winter and summer holidays. Towards the end of the fifties I interrupted my studies for a year to teach in a village school. The next year I was admitted into our district's agricultural school, from which we all went down to a poor county to go in for agriculture in a big way. In the winter of 1961 that school closed down and I was transferred to the agricultural college as a farm worker. I lived near a small town for fourteen years, which covered the Four Clean-ups Movement and the "unprecedented great cultural revolution". I grew vegetables, tended orchards and raised saplings, grew paddy, mended farm tools and minded the store room. I learned basically all kinds of farm work. In those fourteen tumultuous years at the grassroots level I also familiarized myself with the village customs of south Hunan. The ancient flagstone street in this small mountain town, the new grey tiled, red brick houses, the old camphor tree with fine foliage, and the crooked stilt-house all fascinated me and made me feel very close to the past. The vicissitudes, griefs and joys, the funerals and weddings of the local people and even their poultry and dogs made a lasting impression on me. I discovered that though the small town made very slow progress materially in those years, human relations changed incredibly fast. I am glad to have gone through the mill there.

Most authors take up writing mid-way in life, or begin writing in their spare time. When I published my first work in 1962, I was up against the problem of how to handle the relationship between my main job and my spare-time activities. Unless handled correctly it would lead to trouble and hold up my progress in writing. A writer must love life and his own job, otherwise he will feel isolated, unable to integrate with those around him or adjust to his surroundings and create a good environment for his work, study and writing. Because the raw material for a story is the people around you. Then, if you have any profound ideas or original views, these should be expressed in your work. A showy display of brilliance is hard for readers to accept. And overstatements and effusiveness prevent you from thinking deeply about life.

I believe that in life, the soil of literature, there is a dialectical relationship between depth and range, a focal point and the whole spectrum. If a writer produces a certain number of works of a fair standard but confines himself for years to living in one village or grassroots unit, it is bound to restrict his view of life and his artistic vision, bound to reduce his works to mediocre matter-of-fact accounts, as he is unable to draw upon, refine and exploit many valuable materials from life. Thus writers like us who come from grassroots units — especially if we come from villages — are confronted by completely different problems from those writers who seldom go down to the grassroots or only make trips there to collect material. They should settle down there for longer periods, whereas we should try to see more of our country, take part in more cultural conferences, or read more Chinese and foreign masterpieces. I am keenly aware of this from my own experience. After the downfall of the "gang of four" the Writers' Association and other organizations arranged for me to travel widely in China to many famous mountains and great rivers, as well as to attend a course on literature. I was able to read more widely and listen to talks by well-known authors and scholars, to broaden my outlook on life and literature. This travel and study undoubtedly invigorated my writing.

Summing up my experience not long ago I wrote: "In the past few years I have stopped inventing stories and piecing together imaginary episodes, but instead have used the experiences of characters in real life, transforming and refining these to make them typical. This saves trouble. Drawn from life these works have the simplicity and truthfulness of life, not being as contrived as my earlier writing."

Works of literature are the saplings, or sometimes the great trees, a writer raises from the soil of life. Stories like *A Small Town Called Hibiscus* and *The Log Cabin Overgrown with Creepers* were drawn from life then altered and refined. To say "this saves trouble" is not entirely true, for this process of transmutation and refinement is actually more difficult than inventing one's own plot.

My novel *A Small Town Called Hibiscus* appeared in *Modern Times* (Dangdai) No. 1, 1981, and later that year was published by the People's Literature Publishing House. It is based on life but I took pains to alter, amplify and polish it. I first thought of writing this novel in 1979 when I learned about the unjust treatment of a "rich peasant woman" when staying in a county town in the mountains. Hers was a tragic story. A young, hardworking woman during the "hard years", she made enough money selling beancurd to build a storeyed house just before the Four Clean-ups Movement. During that movement she was classified as a new rich peasant and her husband, a timid butcher, hanged himself. Being very superstitious, she thought she had been fated to be the death of her husband, so at night she often went to weep at his grave. Then a prospecting team came to the village and was billeted in her house. One of its technicians was a bachelor in his thirties, and some younger members of the team offered jokingly to arrange for him to marry this young widow. Both were denounced and struggled against, and unable to stand the disgrace he committed suicide too. Convinced that she was ill-fated and had caused the death of an-

other innocent man, the widow went secretly after dark
to weep at the two graves. Not until after the Third
Plenary Session of the Party early in 1979 were wrongs
righted throughout the country, and this widow was
cleared. She realized then that her misfortunes had not
been due to her fate.

This story haunted my mind. But if I wrote it as a
true-life story it could easily be stereotyped, for there
have been so many accounts since ancient times of the
sad fate of women. Several times that year I thought
of writing it but refrained. In 1980, I decided to in-
corporate it in a novel I had long been planning. Then
I gave free rein to my fancy and made up a plot about
a group of people in a small mountain town in four
different periods. By reflecting the local customs and
feelings of that small community in south China, I
hoped to portray that whole turbulent age, now past.
Of course I had set myself a difficult task and might
very easily botch it. I had to draw on virtually all
my experience of village life in the last thirty years, and
I feared my command of language and characteriza-
tion might prove inadequate.

The main characters in *A Small Town Called Hibiscus*
are adaptations of people in real life. Some are based
on several different individuals with whom I lived and
worked for a long time, witnessing all their ups and
downs, their griefs and joys. I also drew on my own
experience. A veteran publisher in Beijing once asked
me: You are relatively young and haven't gone through
great vicissitudes, so how could you enter into the poig-
nant frustration of a woman like Sister Hibiscus? I told
him: I experienced it myself. The strong characters in
life despise weaklings, and the weaklings sympathize

with and feel close to each other, so they can understand feelings which are a closed book to the strong. It is also easy for them to understand the feelings of the strong, because they have so many dealings with them and may be dependent on them.

As for another major character Gu Yanshan, a grassroots Party cadre, while portraying his fine qualities I stressed that he was an "ordinary individual", a stabilizing influence in the small mountain town, looked up to by the townsfolk as their leader; but I did not cover up his weaknesses or the way he vented his feelings. In recent years I have tried to avoid writing in a stereotyped, generalized way, but hitherto I have made very little headway in this respect, and I need to redouble my efforts.

Literature is the product of life. Life is its soil. And the richness or poverty of the soil determines whether a work of literature is vigorous or feeble. A great tree will not grow from barren land; only rich soil and clear water will enable it to flourish.

Looking back at what I have written over the last twenty years I feel ashamed and dismayed. But most writers seem to like to brazen things out with their readers, and so I have written this article to comfort, encourage, mock and explain myself.

**芙 蓉 镇**

古 华

**熊猫丛书**

＊

中国文学出版社出版

（中国北京百万庄路24号）

中国国际图书贸易总公司发行

（中国北京车公庄西路21号）

北京邮政信箱第399号　　邮政编码100044

外文印刷厂印刷

1983年（36开）第1版

1987年第二次印刷

1990年第三次印刷

ＩＳＢＮ 7－5071－0021－9/Ⅰ·22

00650

10—Ｅ—1752Ｐ